Becoming Peacemakers
An Introduction

Becoming Peacemakers
An Introduction

Diane Stanton-Rich

Foreword by Alan Geyer

BRETHREN PRESS
Elgin, Illinois

Becoming Peacemakers.
An Introduction.

Copyright © 1987 by Diane Stanton-Rich

BRETHREN PRESS. 1451 Dundee Avenue,
Elgin, IL 60120.

Cover art by Vista III

The author and publisher are grateful to the holders of copyrighted materials for their permission to use artwork and text reproduced in this volume. The photograph on p. 23 is from the Brethren Historical Library and Archives, Elgin, Illinois. Edward Lee Tucker drew the "Friar Tuck" cartoons on pp. 47, 70, 90 and 97. Bulbul provided the cartoon on p. 86.

Library of Congress Cataloging-in-Publication Data

Stanton-Rich, Diane Karen.
　　Becoming peacemakers.

　　　　Bibliography: p.
　　　　1. Peace — Religious aspects — Christianity.
　　2. Nuclear warfare — religious aspects — Christianity.
　　I. Title.
　　BT736.4.S7 1986　　　　261.8'73　　　　86-20693
　　ISBN 0-87178-937-X

Manufactured in the United States of America

For the sake of the Children . . .

Contents

Part I
The Quest for Peace:
Three Religious Approaches

1. Blessed Are the Peace Makers 13
   Three Christian Attitudes 15

2. Pacifism 19
   Three Historic Peace Churches 20
   Pacifism and Justice 22
   Peace Church Groups Today 24
   Alternative Service 27
   Peace Church Cooperation 29

3. The Crusade 31
   The First Crusades 31
   The Crusade Against Communism 33
   Crusading, Self-Righteous Attitude 35

4. The Just War Theory 39
   The Just War Theory: Pro 39
   The Just War Theory: Con 43

Part II
The Quest for Peace
in the Nuclear Era

5. The Nuclear Era 51
   Nuclear Weapons: A Dramatic Change 51
   Some Technical Considerations 53
   Nuclear War: A Christian Issue 57
   Nuclear Idols 59

6. Three Religious Perspectives on Nuclear War   63
   The Crusade in the Nuclear Era   64
   Pacifism   65
   The Just War and Nuclear Issues   67
   Nuclear Pacifism   71

7. Nuclear Deterrence   75
   Defining Nuclear Deterrence   75
   Limited Nuclear War?   78
   "Star Wars" Technology   80
   Nuclear Deterrence and Fear   83
   The Nuclear Arms Race and the Economy   84

8. Alternatives to the Nuclear Arms Race   87
   Groups Discovering Alternatives   87
   Bowman's Steps to Peace   91
   Civilian-Based Defense   93
   Turning Enemies into Allies   96
   Common Security   99
   The United Nations 101

9. Plans for Action 103
   Action for Individuals 103
   Action for Communities 107
   Prayer 109

Postscript: "A Visit to A Loving and Just Society" . 113

Appendix: Resource Agencies and Organizations . 123

Notes 127

Foreword

For a very long time, from the early 1960s through the 1970s, the churches of America said little and did even less about the escalating nuclear crisis. In the 1970s, both Republican and Democratic administrations were more serious about détente and arms control than were the governing bodies of most churches. Not surprisingly, there was no widespread or mobilized constituency for reversing the arms race or improving US-Soviet relations. The protracted seven-year process of negotiating the SALT II Treaty might have been much less protracted and much more productive had the churches made the nuclear crisis a matter of urgent and steadfast witness. United States Senators who fought long and hard for arms agreements with the USSR reported very little support from the churches or from individual Christians. Indeed, some outstanding Senators were defeated for reelection precisely because of their courageous stands for peacemaking in the face of mean-spirited attacks and the apathy of "good people" — including many Christian folks who remained uninvolved.

Behold! the 1980s present a very different picture. The leadership of nearly every mainline church in America has seriously addressed the nuclear crisis and launched new peacemaking programs. To be sure, physicians and psychologists, scientists and educators, the broadcast media and a galaxy of former government officials have done much to arouse the Christian conscience. Then, too, the very deepening of the crisis—embittered US-USSR relations, rampant military technology, and runaway military spending with its grievous impact on the poor—has stung the souls of millions and helped to generate a peace movement of unprecedented size and range.

All these developments of the 1980s have called forth a vast new literature on nuclear warfare and weapons, the

Soviet Union, and theologies and ethics of peacemaking, as well as practical resources for action.

Diane Stanton-Rich, whose vital vocation as a peacemaker continually developed throughout her years as a college and seminary student, has immersed herself in this new literature. She has composed a very resourceful work which mediates helpfully between theological and technical issues and between scholarly specialists and the educational needs of local congregations. It is both grounded in ethical substance and aimed at practical action. It is lucid in its definitions of Christian witness and alternative policies.

Becoming Peacemakers is, above all, a hope-filled volume which testifies to the kind of rounded, many-sided discipleship now uniquely open to Christians in these days of nuclear cirsis. It dares to imagine that the human family doesn't have to destroy itself and that a loving and just society is, after all, a God-given possibility. I hope Diane Stanton-Rich's book will be put to lively use by hundreds of congregations, groups, and classes. If it is, all of us will have more reason to hope.

Alan Geyer
Churches' Center for
   Theology and Public Policy
Washington, DC

I

The Quest for Peace:
Three Religious Approaches

1

Blessed are the Peace makers: Which Ones?

A Dream
(Sometime in the future . . .)

A vision for repentant churches in the nuclear age
by Jim Wallis

> . . . Used to be that the churches were satisfied with is-
> suing statements and declarations on world peace. Every-
> one knew they didn't mean very much; church members
> were as scared of the Russians as everybody else. Chris-
> tians, too, wanted to hang on to the style of life they had
> become accustomed to in this country. They were as glad
> for the nuclear arsenal as the rest of us, no matter what
> their church offices in New York and Washington said . . .
>
> That was before it all happened. They say it's a revival
> —just like what happened more than a hundred years ago
> when a lot of Christians turned against slavery . . .
> Evangelists are springing up all over. They're preaching
> the gospel and saying that our country's nuclear policy is a
> sin. A sin, mind you, not merely a social or political prob-
> lem.
> It's idolatry, they say, to put your own nation ahead of
> the lives of millions of other people. They're going all over
> the country saying that to turn to Jesus means to turn away
> from nuclear weapons.
> The Christians are no longer happy just to give the
> government good advice about international cooperation.
> They say they must first put their own house in order.
> Pastors are telling people that the Lord wants them to quit
> supporting the arms race. And the people are quitting . . . [1]

Will Christians and churches become involved in working for peace in the way that Jim Wallis describes in "A

Dream"? Many persons would never think of challenging our government's policies as Wallis suggests. They would argue that religion and politics should not mix. Others would say that it is impossible to separate one's faith from one's daily activities as a citizen. Christians have a responsibility to care about those aspects of public life which affect, for good or ill, the welfare of their neighbors.

Theologian Karl Barth said that the Christian meets the world with the Bible in one hand, the daily newspaper in the other. Each hand represents something essential. Christians should live by faith, a loyalty, a commitment coming out of a heritage, but they also should live with an alertness to what is happening in the world right now. Neither faith nor the news alone is enough for responsible decisions because policy decisions take place at the intersection of faith and the contemporary world.[2]

In the Sermon on the Mount Jesus said, "Blessed are the peacemakers, for they shall be called (the children) of God" (Matthew 5:9). Historically, there have been many different approaches to peacemaking. Pacifists, crusaders, and just war advocates argued that they were doing God's will to bring about peace and establish justice. Historically there has always been a tension between these three Christian approaches to making peace. Each approach or perspective uses Scripture to back up its position.

Persons who want to apply Christianity to their citizenship and to war/peace issues are faced with some decisions. When they look to the Bible for guidance, they may become confused because of the varied interpretations given to scriptural passages that refer to war and peace. Some use the Bible to strengthen their claim that war is sinful and a defiance of the righteousness of God as revealed in Jesus Christ. Yet others, in defending a just war, point to the Scripture passage in which Saul is being chastised because, after a particular battle, he did *not* follow the divine command to slay all the men, women, and children of the Amalekites (1 Samuel 15:1-9).

The Bible both condemns and defends violence—even in the New Testament. There are bloodthirsty passages in the Old Testament, such as "Happy shall be he who takes your little ones and dashes them against the rock!" (Psalm 137:9), but there are also passages like "They shall beat their swords into plowshares, and their spears into pruning hooks, nation shall not lift up sword against nation, neither shall they learn war any more" (Isaiah 2:4; see also Micah 4:3). Many of the Old Testament prophets were strong advocates of peace and justice.

There are some passages in the New Testament also that are quoted by people who believe that there are times when it is just to kill or go to war. For example, Jesus is quoted as saying, "I have not come to bring peace, but a sword" (Matthew 10:34), and some of his disciples took swords when they went to the Garden of Gethsemane. Other passages, however, are cited when people are supporting a pacifist position. For example, Jesus tells Peter, "All who take the sword will perish by the sword" (Matthew 25:52), and he says, "Blessed are the peacemakers" (Matthew 5:9). Paul says, "Repay no one evil for evil, but take thought for what is noble in the sight with all" (Romans 12:17, 18).

As Christians have read the Bible and prayed about whether or not they should go to war, there have been no easy answers. Different Christians have come to different conclusions.

Three Christian Attitudes

There has been a struggle over the issues of war and peace within the soul of the church for nearly its entire history, and this struggle cannot be escaped by appealing to the testimony of Scripture alone. Churches certainly have not been united in their approaches to peace. While some have adopted a nonviolent stance, some have advocated violent crusades, and others have tried to justify wars. These three expressions of Christian conscience — pacifism, the crusades, and the just war tradition — have had their theologians, detractors, and sectarian advocates from the beginning. They have all continued to claim the consciences of Christians throughout history, including contemporary variations in the 1980s.

Christian pacifists, notably the Quaker (more formally Society of Friends), the Mennonite, and the Brethren traditions condemn war as un-Christian and refuse on conscientious grounds, to participate in it. Although these "historic peace churches," to which others could be added differ in historical experiences, ethnic origin, and doctrinal emphases, they are united in their conviction that peace is central to the Christian gospel and that war and violence are contradictory to the life and teachings of Jesus Christ.

The Christian crusade, on the other hand, has historically involved an acceptance of whatever kind of force or violence necessary to secure a given end, and the unquestioning participation of the Christian on the assumption that God's will was being served. During the Middle Ages the Church not only justified its decision to go to war against the Turks but also "declared the warfare itself to be a holy cause and a path to sainthood."[3] Today, some official US policy and actions toward Communism, especially after WWII, can be compared to a crusade mentality.

The just war tradition focused on the vindication of justice and the restoration of peace. Peace was valued as an ideal, and recourse to war was a last resort after mediation had failed. Criteria for the just war (summarized in chapter four) set down the conditions under which exceptions to the general obligation of nonviolence might be made. There has been a considerable historical change of definition in the case of just war. The original view of Augustine that violence should almost never be used has been so redefined that people now refer to the just war tradition when trying to justify all kinds of warfare, even warfare that does not fit the just war criteria.

The next few chapters will explore in more detail these three historic Christian approaches to issues of war and peace. The second section of this book will then explain how the presence and build up of nuclear weapons radically has changed the concept of war and has affected profoundly the arguments presented by those who espouse pacifism, the crusade, or the just war tradition. Looking at these Christian approaches in this new light raises questions about nuclear deterrence and about how Christians can find alternatives to the nuclear arms race. People are beginning to discuss, pray about, and develop creative alternatives to the use of nucelar weapons for defense. These alternatives provide the church with hope that some day we will not have to depend on weapons of mass destruction to protect us, and with hope that one day there will be peace.

2

Pacifism

The term "pacifist" has been loosely applied to those who are against war. In many minds it implies vague thinking and do-nothingness. The same can be said of the term "conscientious objector," or "nonresistance." To the Christian a pacifist means one who completely renounces the use of military force and relies on love and nonviolent methods for defense and progress in social change and social justice.[1]

Who are the main historic peace churches and how did they evolve? Is their understanding of Christian pacifism concerned with issues of justice as well as with avoiding lethal violence? What are the historic peace churches doing today about nuclear weapons? How do pacifists view tax resistance and draft resistance?

Three Historic Peace Churches

For nearly 300 years the three traditional peace churches—the Society of Friends, the Mennonites, and the Brethren—have worked together and independently for peace. Though they differ in ethnic origin and doctrinal emphases, they are united in their conviction that peace is the will of God. This shared conviction has led them to a principled resistance to military service and to those institutions and influences which make for violence.[2] Their position might best be called Biblical Pacifism.

These traditional peace groups, which originated in England and Europe, have differed somewhat among themselves in their emphases. The Mennonites (who developed out of the Anabaptist wing of the sixteenth century Protestant Reformation) have been the most aloof from society and averse to participation in government. The English background Society of Friends (Quakers) have been the least segregated from society in general and have been willing to assume political office (as in colonial Pennsylvania) up to the point of war. The Brethren (Church of the Brethren) have taken a median position. Coming out of eighteenth century Pietism, they reflect the tension of "being in the world, but not of it."

The Mennonites made a sharp distinction between the kingdom of the world, which comprised "the unredeemed who live according to the lusts of the flesh and prey upon whom they can,"[3] and the kingdom of Christ. Historically, their view has been that the sword was ordained or created because of sin; in Paradise there was no sword until after the Fall. they have believed that Christ instituted a new order, an order of love and meekness in which there was no constraint. The Christian is a new creature who does not seek retaliation for personal injustices or violence. Mennonites stress obedience, discipline, and the imitation of Christ. Said the converted priest Menno Simons (1496–1561), after whom the group is named:

> Our fortress is Christ, our defense is patience, our sword is the Word of God, and our victory is the sincere, firm, un-

feigned faith in Jesus Christ. Spears and swords of iron we leave to those who, alas, consider human blood and swine's blood well-nigh of equal value.[4]

Despite their small numbers, the Friends have had an important impact in modern religious history. This is largely due to the life of their founder George Fox (1624–1691), the influence of William Penn (1644–1718), the testimony of the Friends against slavery and war, and their notable contributions in reform movements and social work down to the present.[5]

The Friends in England, by their allegiance to conscience, convinced the government of the rights of conscience and for the first time were accorded exemption from military service on this ground in 1802. Earlier, when Fox was offered a captaincy in the Commonwealth army, he refused: "I told them I knew from whence all wars arose, even from the lust, according to James' doctrine; and that I lived in the virtue of that life and power that took away the occasion of all wars."[6] He later said that he had been sent by God to stand as a witness against all violence and to turn people from darkness to light, bringing them from the occasion of war and fighting to the peaceable gospel.

The Brethren originally had two sources for coming to their doctrine of peace nearly 300 years ago: their misery left by the Thirty Years' War (1618–1648), a "religious" contest which devastated Germany; and independent study of the Bible, particularly the New Testament.[7] Traditionally their position has been similar to Mennonite nonresistance. Since 1934, the Church of the Brethren has repeatedly declared that all war is sin. However, they also recognize the right of people to follow individual conscience. Recent statements repeatedly made by the Annual Conferences of the Brethren fit into these categories:

1. Witnessing for peace and against war;
2. Reconciling East-West tensions;
3. Securing world order through a strengthened United Nations;
4. Achieving general and complete disarmament;
5. Structuring positive alternatives to civil defense.[8]

All three of these historically pacifist churches teach that nonviolence starts with a belief in Christ and the ultimate worth of each individual in all lands. They see their task as obedience to Christ through creating a social order in which "the maximum opportunity shall be afforded for the development and enrichment of every human personality."[9] They understand that nonviolence is basically rooted in the recognition that the opponent is human. Being human, opponents will probably react with fear if threatened, but in the long run they are likely to respond with good will if pacifists go out of their way to encourage it. Some might think such a posturing naive. Yet part of Biblical pacifism's goal is to secure an opponent's respect by showing scrupulous care for truth and justice. A Christian pacifist is encouraged to love the enemy, realizing that the enemy is not a villain but a human, a child of God for whom Christ died.

Pacifism and Justice

Biblical pacifism is not unconcerned with the pursuit of justice, as it is sometimes charged. While varieties of pacifism vary, in general pacifists are convinced that nonviolence, suffering love, is the only path to true justice. In contrast, just war theorists believe that a commitment to the pursuit of justice, even by force, is the only path to true peace. The examples of nonviolent activists, like Gandhi and Martin Luther King Jr., provide strong evidence that the commitment to the priority of nonviolence need be neither passive nor ineffective in the face of injustice.

Pacifists believe that nonviolent love is the only effective pathway to the justice of God's kingdom. They point out that violence, even for the cause of justice, breeds hostility and further violence. Violence moves in spiral fashion so that the justice that it temporarily gains risks being wiped out by the greater violence it unleashes. Pacifists remind their critics that Jesus did not resort to violent force in self-defense, even in the defense of justice for the Jewish people under Roman oppression. Pacifists argue that the use of force contradicts the basic strategy for the pursuit of the kingdom of God exemplified in the life of Jesus. God's kingdom cannot be brought about by arms, for violent weapons are themselves sinful obstacles to the coming of God's kingdom.[11]

Brethren Service workers distributing food supplies to *Volksdeutsch* refugees in Austria, 1948.   photo by J. Henry Long

Pacifists believe it is moral to use certain forms of coercion in certain unjust situations, but it is never moral to use killing as a means of coercion. There are no exceptions for this. They believe that people do not have the right to kill any whom God regards as unqualifiedly precious and for whom God suffers in patient love, i.e., to kill anyone. God is never glorified by human violence.[12]

Sometimes pacifists are accused of being unrealistically optimistic about achieving justice without resorting to lethal violence. They claim, however, that once nonviolence is understood, it no longer appears to be naive. A philosophy of nonviolence is a viable alternative and a powerful affirmation of humanity. It is capable of effecting fundamental political, economic, and social changes. Fox himself warned that the cure of war is certainly not as simplistic as the promise not to fight; persons must strive to get at the root of the problem in the human heart.

Peace Church Groups Today

Even though there has been an erosion of the peace witness among the pacifist churches, many have groups and agencies that are quite active today. Examples from the Brethren include the Brethren Peace Fellowship, the "On Earth Peace" Assembly, and the World Ministries Commission of the denomination's General Board. The BPF publishes a newsletter, and distributes "Shalom Tracts" that encourage Christians to resist joining the armed forces.[13] The World Ministries Commission administers such programs as Volunteer Service, Refugee and Disaster ministries, and the offices for a Peace Consultant and International Affairs observer. The Commission seeks to promote peace among all people to work for the relief and rehabilitation of those in distress (particularly the victims of war), to promote better economic and racial relations, and to work in other areas of social need.[14]

The Friends are known the world over for their peace witness. Examples are the Friends Peace Committee and American Friends Service Committee (AFSC). The former distributes pamphlets about peace issues in the same way that the Brethren Peace Fellowship does. The AFSC is based on a profound Quaker belief in the dignity and value of every person and a faith in the power of love and non-violence to bring about change. This conviction is expressed in the committee's action programs: service, development, justice and peace. Perhaps the most visible Mennonite agency working for Peace is the Mennonite Central Committee, a multifaceted relief and development program with projects in many countries of the world. Its "Peace Section" distributes literature, witnesses to governments, conducts peace advocacy, and sponsors other programs.

The historic peace churches have raised for all Christians the issue of war taxes. Every American who pays federal taxes participates in war and war preparation even if only indirectly. This fact is difficult to face when one has a moral commitment to peace. Some Christians feel that they cannot pay for war while working and praying for peace. The demands of conscience outweigh the demands of law and they become war tax resisters.

Early Christians refused to pay taxes for Caesar's temples. Tax resistance was brought to the New World in the seventeenth century by the Quakers. During the Revolution some Brethren and Mennonites also refused to pay taxes for military purposes. Closer to our own time, activists again questioned the unprecedented military spending for World War II and again during the Vietnam War. Currently, war tax resistance continues as a growing response against increased military spending, the nuclear arms build-up, and US foreign interventions. Tax resistance movements are also active in other countries as well. The hope is that war tax resistance on a large enough scale provides a protest which cannot be ignored. Most resisters donate the money to charity that they would have paid in taxes.[15]

Some Christians who are conscientiously opposed to supporting preparation for war with taxes, do not feel that they should refuse to pay all or a major part of their federal income taxes. They may choose, instead, to take a symbolic step such as refusing to pay the federal excise tax on their telephone bills. This telephone tax has been associated with war spending throughout its history. It was first imposed by the War Tax Revenue Act of 1914. Later, during World War II, a 25 percent tax on long distance calls and a 15 percent tax on local service was set up to generate needed federal revenues. The tax was lowered during peace times but increased during the Korean War and the Vietnam War. War tax resisters have continued to consider this telephone excise tax war-related, and its nonpayment an effective and appropriate focus of protest.[16]

Pacifists are not in agreement concerning war taxes. One point of disagreement is whether or not the Bible speaks with one clarity regarding the necessity of tax payment to governments by its citizens. Usually, Matthew 17:24–27, Mark 12:13–17, and Romans 13:1–7 are interpreted as clearly advising Christians to pay all taxes; however, the application of these biblical texts has not always been clear. For example, the first text refers to a temple tax (for maintaining religious institutions) rather than a tax for military uses. In the case of the second text, the oft-quoted render to God and Caesar what belongs to each, it has been argued that Jesus refused to give a simple yes or no to the question. Consequently, some argue that Christians are called in certain situations to make a judgment about what belongs to God and what belongs to the state.

Similarly, Paul's advice to the Romans to "give taxes to whom taxes are due" has been interpreted in different ways. One interpretation of this text is that all taxes should be paid including those for war. However, other interpreters indicate that Paul was talking about paying taxes in a particular time and place, and that in a different situation Paul might not have advised the unconditional payment of taxes. The latter group point to the fact that the early Christians refused to pay taxes for pagan temples.[17]

In the United States today, Biblical pacifists who believe in tax resistance face the dilemma of either violating their conscience by paying taxes they know will go for war preparation or violating the law and enduring the resultant criminal penalties. One solution may be the U.S. Peace Tax Fund. A bill in Congress that would make such a tax fund law has been gaining support over the last several years. Its sponsors believe this fund would do the following:

- reduce the agonizing dilemma facing many conscientious objectors who must presently either disregard their moral beliefs or disobey the laws of the country.
- allocate to the U.S. Peace Tax Fund that portion of the conscientious objector's federal income, estate, and gift taxes which would otherwise be used for military expenditures;
- follow the model of other "trusts" including a board of trustees appointed by the President of the Senate;
- provide funds for development of nonviolent alternatives to conflict (including special projects of the US Institute of Peace).[18]

It would *not* do the following:

- diminish tax obligations, as many current deductions now do. (Participants would still pay 100 percent of their assessed taxes);
- add to current budget deficits or create an unlimited drain on present non-military programs. (A *two* billion dollar cap will provide that a specific amount would go for peace research. Taxes collected above that cap would go to present non-military government programs);
- open the "floodgates" to similar measures for other groups. (Conscientious objection to war is a unique situation which has traditionally been recognized in some manner by the law of this country.)[19]

While pacifists disagree about whether or not it is right to resist paying taxes, most agree that a legal option, such as the World Peace Tax Fund, would be an ideal way to avoid having to pay for war while praying for peace. A catch might be that the government would continue to define "conscientious objection," and thus control who may or may not participate.

Alternative Service

Pacifists in traditional peace churches have long supported those persons who felt it necessary to be conscientious objectors (COs) rather than to participate in war. Of course, not all members of peace churches considered themselves COs and refused to serve in the military forces. However, those who were pacifists struggled to establish legal conscientious objector status. In the late 1930s the peace churches formulated a program for alternative service which was presented to federal authorities. Thus, during World War II the Brethren, Quakers, and Mennonites were able to operate Civilian Public Service camps. Various government agencies took responsibility for work projects (alternative service), while church agencies funded the program and directed camp life. Drafted COs could choose to work in these camps rather than serve in the military.[20]

The peace churches also created in 1941 what is today the National Interreligious Service Board for Religious Objectors to assist draft-age persons of all faiths deal with the

Selective Service system. A related organization, the Central Committee for Conscientious Objectors, was originally founded to help COs who were being prosecuted and imprisoned for failure to register during the 1948 peacetime draft. These and similar groups believe that the right of conscience must be defended against the power of the state. They provide draft counseling, CO literature, and counter recruitment efforts around the country.[21]

The Vietnam War brought public consciousness to yet another aspect of the historic peace church tradition, that of refusal to participate in military service in any form, either as noncombatants *or* through alternative service work. Such noncooperators with Selective Service were frequently arrested. A few served prison terms. Others went to Canada. In some instances the churches themselves were slow to offer support. Following the end of the draft in the 1970s, the issue for some switched to nonregistration with Selective Service. In 1981, a young Brethren college student, Enten Eller, was the first to be convicted, in a highly publicized trial, for nonregistration.

"SOME OF THE MEN DIDN'T WANT TO PARTICIPATE IN THIS SO THEY SPLIT FOR CANADA!"   3/31/72
Doug Marlette, *The Charlotte Observer,* © 1972.

Peace Church Cooperation

The nuclear weapons crisis has brought a new urgency to the witness of the historic peace churches. Mainline churches now want to be "peace" churches. Evangelicals and Catholics have discovered the biblical mandate to be peacemakers. One response of the Quakers, Mennonites, and Brethren to these changing conditions has been to intensify their long standing cooperation through the "New Call to Peacemaking." This loose network of activists has sponsored three national conventions since 1979, and there have also been regional and local gatherings. A quarterly newsletter shares ideas, planning, and support. Although there is no formal national organization, the vitality of this new witness is clear. The Findings Committee from the first national assembly:

> Though we differ in circumstances of historical and ethnic origin and have varied doctrinal emphases we are united in our conviction that peace is the will of God . . . War and violence are denials of the life and teachings of Jesus Christ. The call to peace is central to the Christian Gospel. We believe the time has come for all Christians and people of all faiths to renounce war on religious and moral grounds . . . To these ends we rededicate ourselves with enthusiasm and joy to the Lord's call to be peacemakers. Let us work and witness to the power of reconciling love![22]

3

The Crusade

There is sin and evil in the world," President Reagan said, "and we are enjoined by scripture and the Lord Jesus to oppose it with all our might. Soviet communism is the focus of evil in the modern world . . . and those who favor a mutual freeze on new nuclear weapons ignore the aggressive instincts of an evil empire.[1]

In contrast to Christian pacifists, crusaders have believed that it was God's will for them to kill. Its clearest roots are in the "holy war" of the Old Testament. Though today the US does not kill communists in the same way crusaders killed their victims, there are similarities between the attitudes of the crusaders and the attitudes of those who build up arms to "defend themselves" against communism. Let us first explore the background of the Medieval crusades, then briefly describe the Cold War crusade against communism.

The First Crusades

Participants in the Crusades believed they were fighting in God's war and that God's will was being served. Inspired religious leaders in the Old Testament sent out pieces of flesh to summon the tribes. These leaders asked the will of Yahweh (God) and then led people into battle.

They announced that their God had already delivered the enemy into their hands and that he was with them on the field of battle. They thought of Yahweh as *their* national God rather than the God of all peoples. Later the Ark of the Covenant became a sign for Israel of God's presence. As the ark advanced, Moses cried, "Rise up, Lord, and let thine enemies be scattered," (Numbers 10:35). The leadership of God was revealed in the sense that the war was inaugurated by a God-filled leader, one who spoke for the Lord.[2]

During the Middle Ages, the Christian crusaders had several goals. Perhaps most important was the defeat of the Moslems who threatened Constantinople, and thus Europe. This in turn would save the Byzantine Empire and might serve to reunite the Eastern and Western branches of the Church. Not unimportant was the reconquest of the Holy Land, and in doing so crusaders would be assured of heaven. We do not know whether this last goal was achieved, but we do know that most of the other objectives were achieved only temporarily, if at all.[3]

The first crusaders captured Jerusalem in 1099. In a horrible bloodbath, they killed both defenders and civilians; they raped women and threw infants against walls, and burned down a synagogue filled with Jews who had fled there for refuge.[4]

> Those who embarked on the slaughterous Crusades did so under the motivation of a "Deus vult!" (God will it!). Soon they were sending back reports like this: "In the portico of Solomon, men rode in blood up to their knees and the bridle reins. Indeed, it was a just and splendid judgment of God, that this place should be filled with the blood of the unbelievers when it had suffered so long from their blasphemies."[5]

Two of the scriptural texts that have been used by advocates of the crusades are: 1. the passage in which Jesus cleanses the temple with a whip of cords, a detail mentioned only in John's gospel (John 2:15), and 2. the pronouncement, "I came not to send peace, but a sword," (Matt. 10:34). The first passage shows an instance of fiery indignation against the profanation of the sacred, but, as

Roland Bainton writes in *Christian Attitudes Toward War and Peace,* the whip of cords was no hand grenade, and the success of Jesus in making the temple merchants flee was scarcely due to physical prowess. "For what was one man, even with strands of rope, against such a company. They must have dispersed because they were cowed by a wrath which they recognized as right."[6]

In the second passage, Bainton points out, the word "sword" was used metaphorically, because in the parallel passage in Luke (Luke 12:51) the word "division" is used instead of sword.[17] Other biblical passages used to support the crusades must also be examined more closely.

The crusades were encouraged by people who claimed to have had apocalyptic visions. The "children's crusades" (1212) developed when some youth said that God valued innocence and thus children must play a special role. The Children's Crusade consisted of masses of children and adolescents preparing to go to Jerusalem and defeat the Turks through love, only to die along the way or to be enslaved by those whose territories they crossed. The spirit of the crusades was a constant for centuries, but there were crusades more motable than others; they are called the "Second Crusade," the "Third Crusade," and so forth. Over the centuries, the crusades took many forms. The crusading ideal was used in a variety of circumstances that were quite different from the original intent of retakng the Holy Land.[8]

The Crusade Against Communism

In the twentieth century, many Christians have believed that the evil of fascism or communism is much worse than war itself, and that, sometimes, one must be prepared to fight rather than submit.[9]

The Moral Majority, a part of the current religious right, is helping to lead a US crusade against communism. It is grounded in the following beliefs:

1. America was founded as a Christian nation for a special destiny in the world—it has a divine call.
2. Americans have failed and secular humanism prevails as

a result of the fall of America.
3. America must be restored to its original goals and religious destiny.[10]

Since America is believed to be the country called into being by God to "save the world," it must remain free. The result of this presupposition is a battle between democracy and communism. When religious fundamentalism is wedded to the political right it "baptizes Americanism."[11] It then gives an uncritical affirmation of militarism and a strong defense.

President Reagan allied himself with The Moral Majority's position on communism. His attitudes toward the Soviet Union can be cited as an example of present day crusading spirit. He believes that the Soviet Union is an evil, aggressive empire striving to conquer country after country and spread communist influence across the globe. This belief took hold after World War II, when Reagan headed the Screen Actors Guild during a bitter dispute over Communist influence in the movies.[12] Reagan was also influenced by the Cold War atmosphere. In one of his first press conferences as president, he said of Soviet leaders, "They reserve unto themselves the right to commit any crime, to lie, to cheat."[13]

Reagan has warned that the United States and the Soviet Union are in a "struggle between right and wrong, good and evil."[14] Speaking to the National Association of Evangelicals in Orlando, Florida, in 1983 he said that belief in God should make Americans join him in opposing a nuclear weapons freeze and pressing a vast build-up of US weapons. "There is sin and evil in the world," the president said, "and we are enjoined by scripture and the Lord Jesus to oppose it with all our might."[15]

Helen Caldicott, President of Physicians for Social Responsibility, said about her visit to the White House, "Reagan told me the Russians are totally evil godless communists. When I asked him if he had ever met one, to my surprise he said, 'no'.[16]

Journalist Anthony Lewis criticizes Reagan's attitude and his statement that "belief in God should make Americans join him in opposing a nuclear freeze and pressing a vast build-up of US weapons."[17] Lewis writes that alarm bells should ring when a politician claims that God favors his or her programs. He also criticizes Reagan for applying a black-and-white standard to something that is much more complex. He concludes that it is very dangerous for a president to attack those who disagree with his politics by calling them ungodly.

Because, for many years, The United States has viewed itself as a blessed nation opposing the evils of communism, it built up its nuclear weapons as a means to maintain superiority over the Russians. The Soviet Union also quickly built up its military force and thus the arms race began. Détente during the Nixon, Ford, and Carter administrations had little success easing tensions between the Superpowers, and the poor communication and lack of understanding between the two nations has caused many problems.

Methodist Bishop A. James Armstrong has written:

> Nuclear disarmament is a risk-taking venture. But, how much greater is the risk forced upon us by a mythology that falsely names West "good," and East "evil;" that insists that our security can be found in a balance of nuclear terror or in "winning" an unwinnable nuclear arms race.[18]

Crusading, Self-Righteous Attidude

Daniel Berrigan, in *They Call Us Dead Men*, points out a problem with the self-righteous image most Americans have of themselves. We become the beleaguered defenders of all that is good and noble in life, the society whose interventions are always governed by superior wisdom, whose military might serves only the good of humanity. The US views itself as a peace-loving nation which is the guardian of world peace. The motto of the Pentagon is "peace is our profession." The myth that the United States is perfect suggests that self criticism is difficult and that there is no need to change.

Charles Morrison, author of *The Christian and the War*, also finds fault with the self-righteous attitude of many

Americans. He says that the real error, from the Christian point of view, is that those who maintain a crusade position are not penitent. They see the arms build-up and military strength as the will of God; therefore, they fight (or arm in preparation for fighting) under the great illusion that they are going to accomplish much good by fighting because God is on their side and they're fighting it in obedience to God. They lay the buden of guilt upon the enemy and consider that they are executing divine judgment upon the enemy." There is nothing redemptive, curative, expiatory in this spirit. It carries the seeds of yet more war. There is no cross in it! And there is in it, therefore, no repentance."[19]

In *Violence,* the French lay theologian Jacques Ellul attacks the attitudes of Christians who believe they are doing God's will when they commit acts of violence. Ellul believes violence is never good, legitimate, or "just." He writes that violence is sometimes the order of necessity but that necessity is contradictory to the Christian life, whose root is freedom. When Christians use violence they must realize that they have "fallen back into the realm of necessity; that is, they are no longer the free people God wills and redeemed at great cost."[20]

Ellul goes on to say that the users of violence must not pretend that they are creating order; they must realize they are creating one more injustice. He writes:

> When the Christian uses violence, the Christian knows very well that he is doing wrong, is sinning against the God of Love, and (even if only in appearance) is incresing the world's disorder . . . To fight even the worst of men is still to fight a man, a potential image of God. Thus violence can never be justified or acceptable before God. The Christian can only admit humbly that he could not do otherwise, that he took the easy way and yielded to necessity and the pressures of the world. That is why the Christian, even when he permits himself to use violence in what he considers the best of causes, cannot either feel or say that he is justified; he can only confess that he is a sinner, submit to God's judgment, and hope for grace and forgiveness.[21]

Ellul's attitude is quite a contrast from the self-righteous attitude of crusaders who kill and rape (or build weapons of mass destruction) saying *Deus Vult!" — "God will it!"*

4

The Just War Theory

War is, we have been forced to admit, even in the face of its huge place in our own civilization, an asocial trait . . . if we justify war, it is because all peoples always justify the traits of which they find themselves possessed, not because war will bear an objective examination of its merits.[1]

Just war advocates would choose violence more often than pacifists and less often than crusaders. They do not claim that killing is always wrong, as the pacifists do; yet they do not kill without restraints, as in holy war.

The name "just war" is misleading because it implies that a given war can—objectively and theoretically—be just, that is, war can be viewed as a positive good. Peace Church theologian John Howard Yoder suggests that the following terms more accurately describe what this tradition is about: "war as lesser evil under well-defined circumstances;" "just/unjust-war ethic;" or "justifiable-war tradition."[2] Just war is about the morally permissible use of exceptional, deadly violence in very limited ways.

The Just War Theory: Pro

According to Paul Ramsey, one of the most prominent Protestant supporters of the just war theory, this idea is the "most uninterrupted, longest-continuing study of moral decision-making known in the Western World."[3] The initial object of the just war was the vindication of justice and the restoration of peace; peace was esteemed as an ideal and recourse to war would be used only as a last resort after mediation had failed.

Saint Augustine, one of the first just war theologians, came to the conclusion in the fifth century, that in order for a war to be considered just, certain conditions must be fulfilled. The conditions were as follows:

1. The purpose of the war must be just, e.g., its purpose must not be to satisfy territorial ambition or to exercise power.
2. It must be waged by properly instituted authority (in later centuries, this principle was applied by the powerful in order to claim that they had the right to make war on the powerless but that the opposite was not true).
3. Even in the midst of the violence that is a necessary part of war, the motive of love must be central.[4]

Augustine said, "War and conquest are a sad necessity in the eyes of people of principle, yet it would be still more unfortunate if the unjust should dominate the just."[5]

Just war criteria set down the conditions under which exceptions to the general obligation of nonviolence might be made. Thus, it is a theory of exceptions, marking the outside limit for pluralism in the evaluation of the morality of warfare. Just war thinkers claim that force which violates just war criteria is never legitimate.[6]

Today, depending upon which "expert" one consults, there are from three to fifteen criteria that must be met in order for a war to be considered just. Following are the seven criteria on which most proponents of the just war theory agree:

1. It must be waged for a just cause, such as self-defense, protection of the weak, or honoring treaties. . . .
2. It must not be taken lightly, but only as a last resort. . . .
3. It must have a sincere intention to further what is good, not what is evil. . . .
4. It must not be commenced without the assurance of success, lest all the sacrifice be for nought. In other words, you must not start a war unless you are morally certain you will win it. . . .
5. The principle of "proportionality" must be observed. That is, the evil must not outweigh the good. If victory involves bringing ruination to both sides, or to the human race as a whole, the party with the just cause must forfeit its rights and suffer the evil for the common good. . . .

6. It must be decreed with due solemnity by recognized legal authority. . . .
7. It must be conducted in a "civilized manner." Above all, innocent civilians must be protected.[7]

Both pacifists and just war Christians have a distrust of violence. The just war tradition, like pacifism, regards war as evil. The traditions differ in their understandings of the nature of the Christian moral obligation to avoid war. For the pacifist, this obligation is more or less absolute, but for the just war advocate it is conditional and can be overridden in certain circumstances. They differ in their understandings of how Christians should respond when the values of respect for human life and the preservation of peace conflict with the values of justice and human freedom. Just war theorists would argue that sometimes a society must use violence, including deadly violence, in order to protect justice and freedom. They feel that some forms of injustice are so serious that they undermine the very possibility of true peace. Peace and justice are interdependent, and justice is regarded as the precondition of peace in the concrete political order. Thus the pursuit of justice, even by violence, can in some circumstances be the only way to fulfill the duty to promote both peace and justice.[8]

Just war thinking appeals to the biblical sources of Christian faith that show that justice is a precondition for genuine peace. It points to the biblical affirmation that the human community is deeply distorted by human arrogance and sin. Thus conflicts between the demands of justice and the sanctity of human life are to be expected. The just war theory presupposes the nonviolent example and teaching of Jesus, but it also points to the commitment to justice in biblical faith. It argues that pacifism absolutizes the value of human life at the expense of other values such as justice, freedom, and human rights. It also claims that pacifism rests on a one-sided reading of the biblical sources.[9]

Just war thinkers share the pacifist abhorrence of violence and even agree that violence tends to breed violence. However, in order to check escalating violence society must set up criteria that control it in the short run and establish just and peaceful conditions in the long run. For example, by meeting Nazism with counterviolence, just war thinkers argue, WWII prevented a ghastly future for even more millions.[10]

Just war theorists argue that pacifism cannot be the policy of a government. This is because a government by its very nature is a trustee for the security and freedom of a nation, and there is no pacifist nation. Even nations that have almost no armaments depend upon protection, typically by a more powerful neighbor, that might involve the use of military force. Just war theorists also criticize pacifists for being naive:

> [They] . . . fail to do justice to the need to prevent a monopoly of military power in any nation or group of nations. They tend to play down the implacable character of some aggressive or tyrannical forces that threaten. They trust too much in the power of persuasion, the persuasion of loving example, to resist such evil forces.[11]

As well as finding fault with pacifism, just war theorists believe that the crusades certainly should not be a model for government policies. One of their major differences with such a model is that just war theorists do not believe people possess the ability to decide which nation or regime is the one (if there is one) which is just. Just war theorists do not claim, as the crusaders did, that God is only on their side and that they are morally right and the other side is wrong. Instead of telling persons which side is just, the just war guidelines tell people what moral limits should be followed.

Dietrich Bonhoeffer, the German theologian executed by the Nazis, has inspired some just war theorists. He was a young German pastor who participated in the attempted assasination of Hitler. Bonhoeffer wrote that it was his Christian duty to try to kill Hitler. He felt it was "just" to fight evil, such as the evil Hitler was perpetrating, with violence. "If you see a mad dog coming down the road, you shoot him to protect the innocent."[12]

Paul Ramsey claims that *love* must be the guide when deciding if a war is just or unjust and that love permits everything, even violence: "Everything is quite lawful, absolutely everything is permitted which love permits, everything without a single exception . . . Therefore, the Christian is permitted to use force, nay, even positively obliged to do so."[13]

Though Ramsey says love permits everything, he also says that love limits the use of violence by prohibiting the killing of any person not directly or closely cooperating in the force that should be repelled: "Christian love should again, as in the past, surround the little ones with moral immunity from direct killing. It should discern the difference between just war and murder."[14]

The nature of war, of course, has changed since the time of Augustine. Modern war employs weapons of mass destruction. It is "total war" in the sense that entire populations and the economies of the warring states are committed to the conflict. Ramsey concludes that the Christian cannot approve of strategic bombing of whole civilian populations and that it is never right to intend to directly kill millions of children in order to get at their fathers. The work of love, in limiting the conduct of war, creates the rule of "double effect," which is the prohibiting of direct and intentional killing of anyone besides combatants in warfare. He claims that the just war doctrine is not only applicable today but that to depart from it is "to surrender it to irrationality and gross immorality."[15]

The Just War Theory: Con

In his article in *The Michigan Christian Advocate,* Donald Strobe analyzes the just war rationale. He addresses seven criteria upon which most proponents of the just war theory agree. Of these Strobe criticizes the first criterion (it must be waged for a just cause, such as self-defense, protection of the weak, or honoring treaties), the third criterion (it must have a sincere intention to further what is good, not what is evil), and the fourth criterion (you must not start a war unless you are morally certain you will

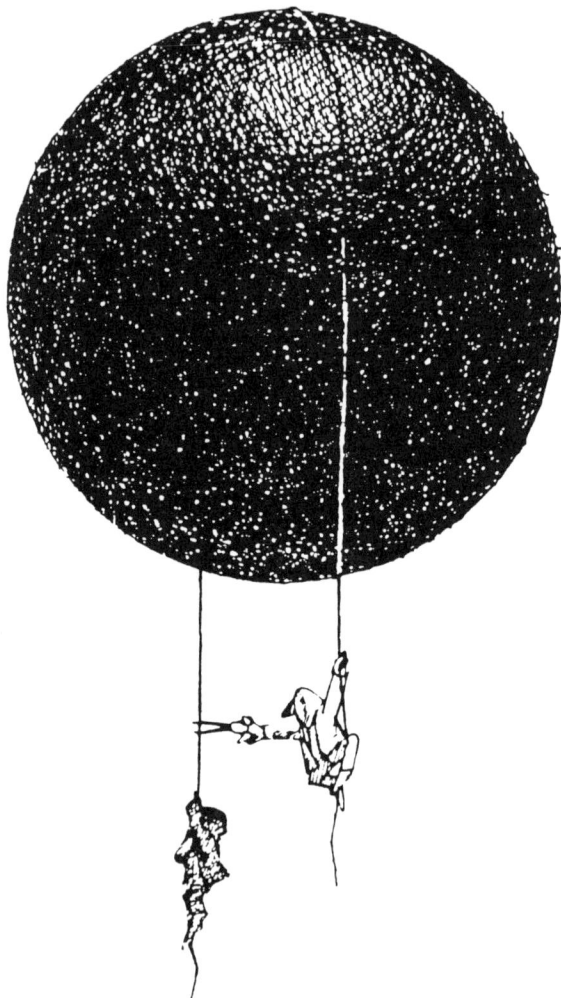

win it).[16]

Concerning the first condition, Strobe comments that in actual practice every nation believes that it is the just nation and that the other nation was at fault. Through more than sixteen centuries, no church or state that subscribed to the just war tradition has ever claimed that a war fought from its side is unjust and should not be waged. In commenting on the third criterion, he writes that no one ever admits to themselves or to others that they are doing evil. People convince themselves that evil is good, and then they set about doing it. Finally, with regard to condition number four, Strobe implies that it is impossible to be absolutely certain that you will win a military contest. There are countless examples of nations that went into war believing that they would win but ended up losing.[17]

Jacques Ellul, author of *Violence,* also finds fault with the just war theory. He is critical of its idea of the lesser evil, that war is legitimate as an extreme means of preventing greater evil for humanity. Ellul criticizes this by pointing out that what is the greater evil is defined differently by different groups. For example, some Christian groups claim that the greater evil is communism, others claim it is the exploitation of the third world by the capitalist nations.

Ellul criticizes the following just war view that Christians should kill the enemy without hating: "We are forced to go to war; we must accept war because, according to Christian teaching, we must obey the state; but the Christian, as Christian, will engage in war without hating his foes; he will kill the enemy but he will not hate him."[18]

This is considered the "Christian paradox" because loving the enemy while acting cruelly toward him or her seems impossible. Ellul points out that the heat of battle and the violence of combat rule out any thought or emotion except the consciousness of "kill or be killed." He also argues that current long-distance nuclear weapons, designed for the collective destruction of a far-off enemy, rule out love.[19]

Later in *Violence,* Ellul writes that the term "just violence" is totally absurd. Those who say that unjust violence can be repelled only by just violence enter into a vicious circle—for violence corrupts the best of ends and it has no limits. Institutions established through "just" violence are never an improvement.[20]

He also criticizes those who maintain that "violence must be condoned as a means of combating social injustice or of coping with the violence of others—provided, however, that it be used for the benefit of others, not for that of its practitioner."[21]

Ellul claims that this requires an impossible sequence of events because one would have to be able to measure out exactly the amount of violence needed in order to achieve the desired just result. One would, in effect, have to compute the following: "The evil I want to inflict on the other (who is bad, either because of his personal qualities or because he belongs to a certain race, class, or nation or holds certain opinions) — is the evil I inflict justified by the evil he has done?"[22]

How is a nation to know that, at the very least, the violence it commits is not worse and more far-reaching than the violence committed by its enemy?

Ellul's final argument against the belief that violence can be just is his observation that violence is contagious because of its long-lasting effects on the victims. They carry the effects on their body and in their hearts and sub-consciouses for years. Revenge becomes very important. The reality is that violence breeds violence.

There has been considerable historical alteration in making the case for the just war. Its clear presumption against even exceptional violence has so changed that people now refer to the just war tradition when trying to justify all kinds of warfare, even nuclear warfare that in no circumstance fits the classic just war criteria. Persons who now talk the just war theory often have lost sight of its original questions that presumed not fighting as the norm: "May a Christian ever take part in lethal violence against another of God's children?" and "Is fighting in war always a sin?"[23]

Instead of considering nonviolence the norm, some try to use the just war idea to justify the use of aggression and preemption rather than self-defense. John Howard Yoder said, "The shell [of the just war tradition] has been retained, while what goes on beneath it is something quite different from what the theologians who initially found the just war tradition convincing could ever have meant or would ever have approved."[24]

This section has briefly looked at Christian pacifism, the crusades, and the just war tradition. Part II will examine how these religious perspectives on war and peace are affected by the nuclear era. The fact that we now live in an age in which the world has enough nuclear power to destroy itself many times over; the fact that we can no longer expect war to have limits to the amount of destruction it can cause; the fact that even a "limited" nuclear war would be drastically different from other wars humanity has known — these conditions have an effect on the traditional religious ways of viewing war and peace.

II

The Quest for Peace:
in the Nuclear Era

5

The Nuclear Era

Humankind is entering a period of unique opportunity and unprecedented danger.[1]

This chapter will look at the drastic change in the concept of war now that nuclear weapons exist, some technical aspects of nuclear weapons, the concept that nuclear war is a crucial issue with which all Christians must be concerned, and some of the ways in which nuclear weapons are, in fact, idolatrous.

Nuclear Weapons: A Dramatic Change

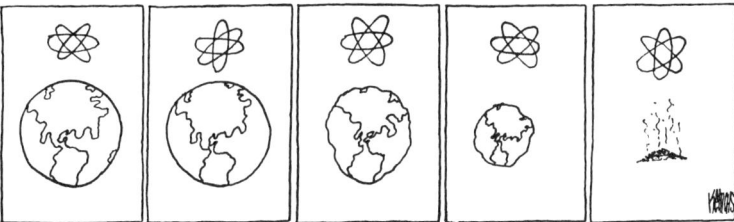

Many people have strong feelings concerning this new age which has been created by nuclear technology and weapons. The following quotes provide a few examples:

The mushroom-like clouds that rose from the ruins of Hiroshima and Nagasaki a (short time) ago ushered in a new age in the life of mankind. Not only must we come to terms with the fact that all civilized life upon this planet may come to an end but that this is possible through human decision and action.[2]

[The development of nuclear weapons] has catapulted us into an era of much greater risk than before; we have developed a technology that is capable of ending modern civilization.[3]

The word "war" to which we have become accustomed in the past, is no longer adequate to describe what we can expect, but we have no better word. We can call it "nuclear war," and we must learn to feel how different nuclear war is likely to be from wars with chemical explosives which mankind has survived in the past.[4]

Although war is quite different now that there are nuclear weapons, some military strategies do not seem to reflect this change. Einstein said, "When we released the energy from the atom everything changed except our way of thinking. Because of that we drift towards unparalleled disaster."[5]

Einstein was partially referring to the way in which people, including military advisors, still look upon war as a conflict between two or more armies. Americans, especially it seems, have romanticised views of our own Civil War (1861-1865) with gallant men in Blue or Gray competing for a field of honor. All that has changed. The speed and total penetrability of a nuclear strike would be so different for both the military and civilians from past wars that the word "war" itself may be misleading. There really is no defense against the destructiveness of nuclear weapons.

Because nuclear war is so different from anything in the past, there is a tendancy for people to be guided by their emotions rather than by reason when they confront this issue. On one hand, people declare fearfully that there is no evil greater than the risk of nuclear war; and on the other hand, some speak recklessly of preventive war and of massive retaliation. Both positions spring from fear rather than reason. A second tendency is for people to oversimplify the nuclear issues, grasping any program which promises easy answers; or for ordinary people to feel that the issues are too complex so they cannot do anything about it. A final tendency is for people either to grow so accustomed to the current "balance of terror" that a sense of urgency is lost, or to become so pessimistic that they are swamped with feelings of helplessness and hopelessness.

In an attempt to deal with the possibility of nuclear war on a rational level, it may be helpful to look at some of the technical aspects of such weapons.

Some Technical Considerations

Since 1945 the United States and the Soviet Union have gone from one nuclear weapon between them to nearly fifty thousand. The best and the brightest minds cannot agree on why there must be an arms race. There is no widely accepted explanation of why the United States and the Soviet Union, who for four years combined their efforts to defeat a common Nazi enemy have now assembled a nuclear weapons capability that would enable each to destroy the other many times over.[6] Ideology seems a poor excuse.

In thirty minutes, a fraction of these fifty thousand nuclear weapons can destroy every city in the northern hemisphere. Yet the US and USSR plan to build over 20,000 more nuclear weapons and a new generation of nuclear missiles and aircraft over the next decade.

If the nuclear race is not stopped, then Counterforce and other "nuclear warfighting" systems will improve the ability of the US and USSR to attack the opponent's nuclear forces and other military targets. This will make both sides more likely to use these weapons in a crisis rather than risk losing them in a first strike. Such developments encourage hairtrigger readiness for a massive nuclear exchange.[7]

Hairtrigger readiness would increase the chances of a nuclear accident because a nuclear war could be started by computer error. James Muller reported that during a ten month period, North American Defense Command had 151 false alarms due to mechanical and human errors which could have resulted in a nuclear catastrophe.[8]

Reflecting on this problem of hairtrigger readiness (also known as launch-on-warning), Oren Chamberlain, one of the scientists on the Manhattan project that began the development of nuclear weapons, wrote:

If the Soviets, for example, suffered the same kind of computer error that we in this country have experienced with respect to nuclear weapons, after our deploying the Pershing II missile, they might be forced to make a four-minute decision to launch their nuclear weapons, thus destroying, say, 20 cities from San Francisco to Washington, D.C. in retaliation to an imagined U.S. strike.[9]

Two examples of weapons which encourage hair-trigger readiness are the US Pershing II and cruise missiles (which have a brief flight time and are difficult to detect). The US deployment of these missiles into Europe could be extremely dangerous because if the Soviets have reason to think a NATO attack has begun, they will need to decide whether to launch their own missiles or lose them. Thus, the risk of an accidental nuclear war is increased.

It is more difficult to verify these new missiles because they are small, mobile, and easy to conceal. Since these weapons cannot be monitored with confidence, it will be difficult to have an arms control agreement. Like the US, the Soviets probably will not sign treaties which have major verifications problems. Unless the nuclear arms race is halted, the danger of nuclear war will be greater in the latter part of the twentieth century than ever before.

To get a better picture of how destructive nuclear weapons can be, *Nuclear Disaster,* by Tom Stonier, provides a sobering description. Stonier details what would happen if a 20-megaton nuclear weapon was detonated in the center of New York City. The first result would be the death of ten times as many people as were killed in all the wars in American history. Seven million people would die from firestorm, blast, and radiation. Within a ten mile radius, all living things would die. Trucks and automobiles would be hurled about. Winds pushed outward would create a huge vacuum at the center that would begin to draw the winds back at speeds up to 125 miles per hour. Houses and other objects caught in this double pressure would be blasted from both sides. A fireball would form, its heat so intense that humans 40 miles away would receive second degree burns. People looking at the fireball 250 miles away would suffer severe eye damage.[10]

Firepower
to Destroy a World

The dot in the center square represents all the firepower of World War II—3 megatons. The other dots represent the firepower in existing nuclear weapons—18,000 megatons (equal to 6,000 WW IIs). About half belong to the Soviet Union, the other half to the U.S.

The top left circle represents the weapons on just one Poseidon submarine—9 megatons (equal to the firepower of 3 WW IIs) enough to destroy over 200 of the largest Soviet cities. The U.S. has 31 such subs and 10 similar Polaris subs. The lower left circle represents one new Trident sub—24 megatons (equal to the firepower of 8 WW IIs)—enough to destroy every major city in the northern hemisphere. The Soviets have similar levels of destructive power.

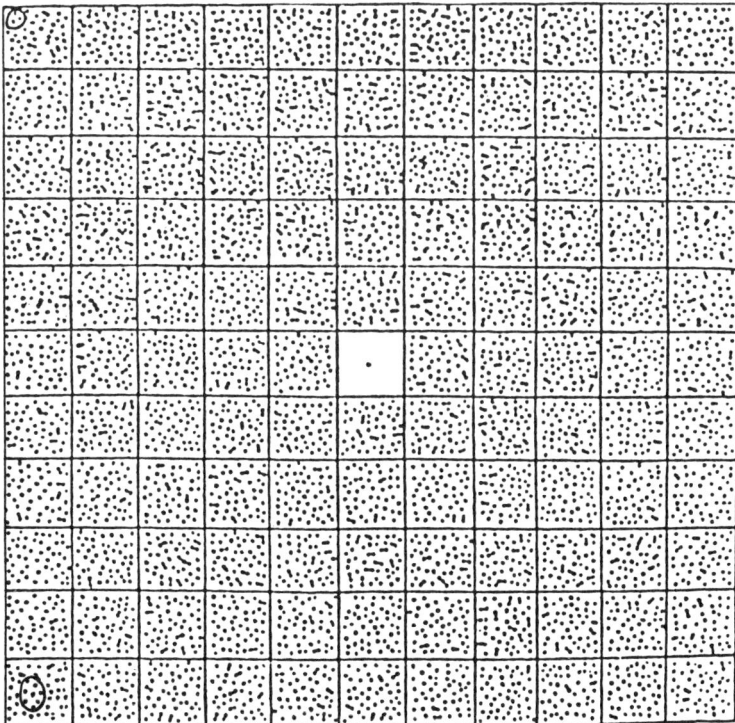

These are only a few of the devastating effects of a nuclear explosion. After the explosion there would be terrible effects on the entire ecological system and the balance of nature. Norman Thomas said, "Survivors of thermonuclear war, if such there are, will envy the dead."[11]

To make a point about the excess of nuclear weapons, John Stott described the nuclear power on Poseiden submarines: "Each Poseiden submarine has 10 missiles, each of which has 14 MIRV warheads, each of which is equivalent to the Hiroshima's. America's 11,000 nuclear warheads could annihilate the complete world population 12 times over."[12]

Such overkill and the arms race itself can be viewed in a rather comic way. It is as if the US and the USSR are locked in a room together, and have doused one another with gasoline, and are each feverishly racing against the other to perfect the best cigarette lighter with which to set the other on fire. They call it "Mutually Assured Destruction" (MAD). This seems crazy, but no less so than the arms race.[13]

George Kennan, one of the architects of the postwar World War II "containment" policy towards the Soviet Union, recently wrote: "We have gone on piling.weapon upon weapon, missile upon missile, new levels of destructiveness upon old ones. We have done this helplessly, almost involuntarily . . . like men in a dream, like lemmings headed for the sea."[14]

The proliferation of nuclear weapons is an important problem. As of 1982, the US, USSR, United Kingdom, France, and China had deployed nuclear weapons, and other nations were rapidly developing the ability to do the same. India, Israel, and South Africa are widely believed to possess nuclear weapons or the ability to assemble them on short notice. The technology is becoming available, even to Third World countries and terrorist organizations. There are many reasons why nations want "the bomb": prestige, political clout, fear of attack, blackmail, terrorism, and so on. The more the nuclear powers expand their arsenals, the more likely it becomes that other countries will find compelling reasons to initiate their own nuclear weapon programs. The prospects for a major expansion of the nuclear arms race remain alarming.[15]

Nuclear War: A Christian Issue

Nuclear war is a crucial issue with which Christians must be concerned. Nuclear war is sinful. It has the potential to destroy all of God's creation, and it is based on the theory that to kill is better than to be killed. Thus it contradicts the Christian idea of "turning the other cheek." Would not the teaching of Jesus be that it is better to perish as the victim of the inhumanity of others, rather than to save oneself or one's nation by making others the victims of one's own inhuman acts.[16]

Jim Wallis, in *The Call to Conversion: Recovering the Gospel for These Times,* compares nuclear weapons to slavery. First he reminds us of the decades leading up to the American Civil War during which time there was a religious revival in this country. Opposition to slavery was central to the revival and was seen as a fruit of conversion. The Christians felt that treating people as property was an abomination to God and a monstrous system that had to be stopped as a matter of faith.[17]

Wallis writes that slavery was an overarching moral question that intruded upon the routine of the church's life and pleaded for the compassion and the courage of God's people everywhere. Like slavery, acceptance of nuclear weapons today has intruded upon our church's life and has brought us to a crisis of faith. He states:

> The nuclear threat is no more just a political issue than slavery was; it is a question that challenges everything we say about our faith in God and our allegiance to Jesus Christ. In other words, the growing prospect of nuclear war presents us with more than a test of our survival; it confronts us with a test of our conversion.[18]

Another moral question that must be asked is what values are expressed when a government chooses to spend massive amounts of money on war machines. In the American context, military spending takes money away from humanitarian programs. Resources, including raw materials, money, human time and energy, are often used for military purposes when they could be used to address human needs. Martin Luther King Jr. said that a nation which spends more money on the military than on programs for social improvement is approaching spiritual death.

Military spending creates far fewer jobs than almost any other kind of public or private spending:

Jobs Per Billion Dollars (in 1980 $)

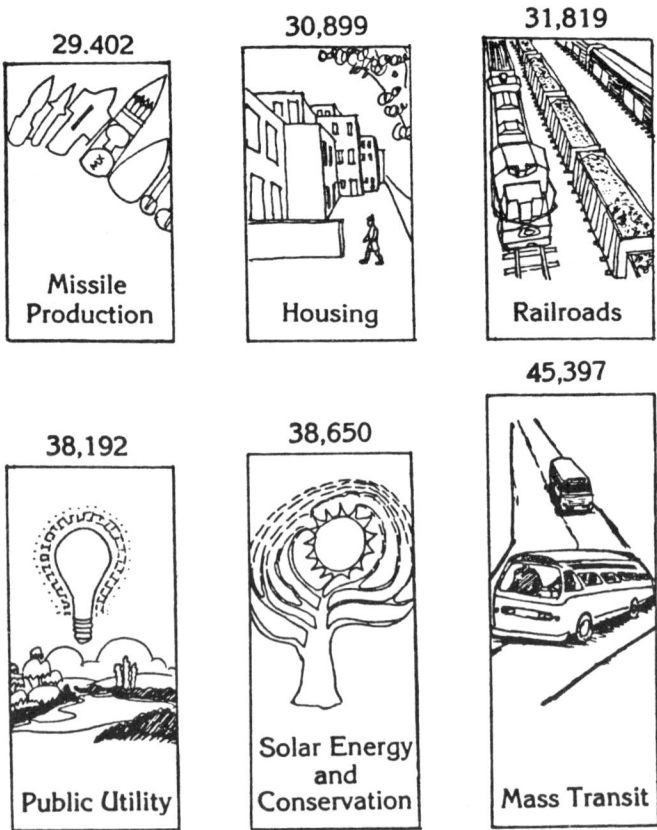

29.402

Missile Production

30,899

Housing

31,819

Railroads

38,192

Public Utility

38,650

Solar Energy and Conservation

45,397

Mass Transit

A few companies have decided to shift toward "peace conversion," that is, manufacturing items for civilian use instead of building the military goods that they used to produce. For example, a factory that made weapon parts could build parts for other industries such as transportation. Employment need not be dependent upon a war economy. Our society needs an economic conversion from a permanent economy built on military defense spending to one of producing goods and services to meet human needs.

According to the New Abolitionist Covenant promoted by many peace organizations, nuclear weapons are morally unacceptable and the growing prospect of nuclear war presents society with more than a test of survival; it confronts the church with a test of faith. Nuclear war is a crucial issue about which Christians must be concerned.

Nuclear Idols
A Christmas Eve Dream

When the organ grew quiet, the robed minister walked to the altar and read these words:
> *The nuclear bomb is our shepherd,*
> *we shall not object;*
> *It makes us lie down in deep shelters.*
> *It leads us unto the brink of war;*
> *but it restores our strength.*
> *It leads us in the paths of nuclear*
> *escalation for its name's sake.*

> *Even though we march through the dust*
> *of nuclear fall-out,*
> *We fear no enemy,*
> *For the Pentagon is with us;*
> *its MX and Pershing missiles,*
> *they comfort us.*

The Bomb prepares a holocaust for us
in the cities of our enemies;
It anoints our lands with missiles,
our silos overflow.
Surely victory and democracy shall be
with us all the seconds of our lives;
And we shall dwell in the shadows of
the silos till life be no more.

> Then with one voice the congregation re-
>   sponded:
> Holy, holy, holy Lord,
> God of power and might,
> Heaven and earth are full of your glory.
> Hosanna in the highest.
> Blessed is the Bomb
> which comes in the name of the Lord.
> Hosanna in the highest.
> —C. David Hainer[19]

Nuclear weapons are modern day idols. People put their faith and trust in "the almighty bomb" to save them from destruction. If nuclear weapons are the foundation of national security, they also have become "false gods" to the nuclear powers. Biblical faith shows that God is all powerful and that God's supreme act of love was the sending of Jesus who was among us defenselessly. Jesus said, "Fear not those who kill the body and after have nothing they can do." The ultimate security for Christians is peace in Christ.[20]

Of course, things are not quite this simple. People derive their sense of security in this life from a combination of factors: adequate income, physical comforts, stable personal relationships, faith in God, sustained employment, national security, as well as others. Some people feel that arms supremacy is necessary for them to feel safe in other areas.

What has ultimate value? The scriptures clearly teach that material possessions are not ends in themselves. Those who would protect property at all costs must ask themselves whether they have more trust in God, or in the bomb. Do they confess Jesus as Lord and yet depend on nuclear weapons instead to protect their life and possessions? If so, there is a conflict. Conversion in our day must include turning away from the idols of nuclear weapons as we turn to Jesus Christ. Building up nuclear weapons is idolatrous because it is putting things—material possessions, the nation, and military power—before God.

Some might argue that "this is fine for a personal ethic, but can Christians expect the US government, or any government, to say absolutely "In God We Trust"? The real question, however, is the degree to which Christians must submit to a state whose policies are unjust, or evil, or contrary to God's will. Anne Meyer writes that Americans should not make an idol of our nation. God does not favor the United States above all others and we do not have the "right" to control what other nations do, by economic or military means, in order to serve our own self-interest.

With respect to military power before God, people need to recognize that, in effect, this is worship of the power of death instead of the power of love.[21] We would do well to remember the words of James 4:1, 2: "Where do all the fights and quarrels among you come from? . . . You want things, but you cannot have them, so you are ready to kill; you strongly desire things, but you cannot get them so you quarrel and fight." Our nation and others have too often resorted to military action in order to secure wealth, protect industrial capacity, and insure world-wide multi-national operations. We are willing to fight and kill rather than give up resources that we consider to be ours.

There is hope, however, as people begin to place their trust more fully in God's care for them. With less complicity in the security of armaments, their circle of concern expands from the narrow confines of themselves and their nation to the world. It is then that they realize that to work for peace is to understand the true security which Christ brings, and they are ready to join him in this work.

6
Three Religious Perspectives on Nuclear War

Nuclear weapons explode the theory of just war. They are the first of (humanity's) technological innovations that are simply not encompassable within the familiar moral world . . . Nuclear war is and will remain morally unacceptable, and there is no case for its rehabilitation.[1]

"NO, I'M NOT WORRIED ABOUT NUCLEAR WAR.
I'VE GOT MY OWN PROBLEMS!"

In what ways has the introduction of nuclear weapons affected or altered the traditional perspective of the crusaders, pacifists, and just war advocates? Will pacifists and just war defenders come to agree with each other that it is immoral to use nuclear weapons?

The Crusade in the Nuclear Era

The Moral Majority speaks about the need for nuclear weapons so that the US, "God's country," can maintain "peace through strength." Persons who talk about peace through strength often claim that the US is presently "behind" the Soviet Union in overall military strength. Therefore the US must build up its nuclear arms. They encourage citizens to believe that American arms are inferior and that America should spend trillions of dollars on the arms race. They attack the position that there should be a bilateral US/USSR nuclear weapons freeze, claiming such a freeze would leave the US vulnerable.

However, contrary to the above argument, the Center for Defense Information in Washington, DC writes that American weapons are not inferior to that of the Soviet Union:

> The United States and the Soviet Union today possess far more than enough nuclear warheads to destroy each other many times over. It does not matter who attacks first and who retaliates. Both sides will be destroyed.

> The US has MORE total nuclear weapons, MORE strategic weapons, MORE nuclear weapons on submarines, and MORE nuclear weapons on bombers than the Soviet Union. US weapons systems are generally more reliable and accurate than Soviet weapons systems.

> The Soviet Union has more nuclear weapons on land-based missiles (ICBMs) than the US. This one area of Soviet advantage is more than compensated for by the many areas of US superiority.[2]

Are Americans "better dead than Red" or "better Red

than dead?" The political Right claims that it is essential that citizens be unquestionably willing to risk their lives for the defeat of communism. They point out that Americans owe their freedom to their fathers who believed that liberty was worth fighting for, even to the death. The "Left" counters with, "What is the use of fighting against communism if the result is mutual suicide?"

John Bennett wrote that the rhetoric "better dead than Red" and its counterpart are not even appropriate to today's situation. Changes and divisions within the international Marxist-Leninist movement make the old "red or dead" contrast quite meaningless today. There is no monolithic communist threat. There are Yugoslav "red," Chinese "red," Stalinist "red," with some socialist states squared off against each other. Today one is not choosing between death and a permanent centralized Stalinist slavery.[3]

Christians in almost every war since pacifism was rejected as an ideal rather than an ethical norm have killed and been killed in conflicts that reflect more the crusade pattern rather than the just-war tradition. Leaders have tried to cover and interpret crusade-like wars with the rhetoric of the just-war theory. Still, most Christians in Europe and America believe that the just-war tradition has better moral guidance than the crusades. The traditional just-war position would have rejected some of the crusade-style wars that have been fought under the guise of just-war rhetoric.

Pacifism

The historic biblically pacifist position has changed little with the introduction of nuclear weapons. This is because such pacifism is rooted in an expectation of discipleship, not a political or military situation. Of course, pacifists are against nuclear war as much as they are against all warfare. They speak out directly against nuclear weapons in many ways. Note, for example, this passage from a Mennonite Central Committee pamphlet:

1. We believe that the concept of nuclear deterrence, which involves a trust in nuclear weapons, is a form of idolatry.

2. We call upon all people and nations to renounce the research, development, testing, production, deployment and actual use of nuclear weapons, and commit ourselves to resist these activities in the United States. We call for the conversion of jobs in science and industry from warmaking to peacemaking purposes.
3. We identify consumerism, excessive patriotism, and fear as major reasons for support of the arms race in American society. We call upon Mennonite and Brethren in Christ congregations to discern the evidence of these trans-gressions in their midst and to lead believers into an alter-native experience of simplicity, community, and faith in the body of Christ.[4]

Jim Wallis points out that the sign of the nuclear age is the Bomb; whereas the sign of Christ is the Cross. The Bomb threatens to undo the work of the Cross by destroying, mak-ing violence victorious, giving evil dominion, allowing death to reign supreme. Pacifists ask, "Will we choose to live under the sign of the Cross or the sign of the Bomb? . . . The great evangelistic task before us is to convert people from the Bomb to the Cross."[5]

In the grim reality of nuclear weapoons lurks a remark-able resemblance to pagan idols as described in the Bible. Psalm 115 elaborates on the senselessness of idols that have

> noses, but never smell
> hands, but never touch,
> feet, but never walk.

It concludes "Their makers will end up like them, and so will anyone who relies on them." Like these idols, the bombs that nuclear weapons carry have no feeling, no con-science, no imaginative sensitivity for the human beings toward whom they are targeted.

When people absolutize their nation, they are behav-ing like the people in biblical times who tried to worship the Lord God (Yahweh) and other gods at the same time. People depend on God to save them, but they also feel the need to give the nation-state its due in terms of full allegiance, support of military defense, and readiness to kill and be killed in war. They try to praise God and to praise military nationalism both.

Biblical pacifists point out that no one can serve two masters. Now, more than ever, there is a need for those who reject all forms of violence.

The Just War and Nuclear Issues

When applying just war criteria to the nuclear era, many observers conclude that the use of nuclear weapons cannot be condoned. This section will first survey the ideas of Paul Ramsey who maintains that there can be a just nuclear war. It will then look at the reasons why the use of nuclear weapons is not morally acceptable according to the just war tradition.

Justification for Nuclear Weapons

Paul Ramsey argues that a limited nuclear war can fit the criteria of the just war theorists. He claims that the just war theory supports certain types of nuclear deterrence. He writes that people are becoming too emotional about the nuclear issue and that they do not realize that there can be limited nuclear exchanges which will not cause total destruction. The key is that nuclear war can and must be limited. Ramsey says that the military should make preparations for limited nuclear war to solve the dilemma that although violence is absurd, force is necessary to achieve political ends. Politics needs force, but morals condemn violence. The solution to this dilemma, he says, is in limiting and controlling the use of violence.[6]

Ramsey writes that it is the task of military strategists and tacticians to contain the use of force to the minimum necessary for accomplishing "the multiple ideas inherent in the moral idea of war."[7] Thus, he points out, even in the nuclear age, it is possible to draw the line between appropriate military action and the sheer massacre of civilian populations. When nuclear war comes, humanity should be prepared to conduct it justly.

Along the same lines, Ramsey writes that it is "civilized warfare" rather than pacifism or a dread of weapons that is needed in today's society. Civilized warfare would seek to limit the conduct of war to means intended only to repel military force. It would keep nations from intentional killing of a million school children in order to punish their fathers.[8]

He makes a further distinction between the morality of strategic bombing and of tactical bombing. In both cases, the innocent are killed. However, in strategic bombing, death to the innocent is done directly and is clearly wrong. In tactical bombing, death of the innocent is indirect (only the military target is attacked directly). Ramsey suggests that in tactical bombing the unavoidable and foreknown death of the innocent is not the direct objective and thus is a "regrettably necessary secondary effect of action justifiable in itself."[9]

Paul Ramsey claims that people find it easier to plan murder and mutual suicide rather than defense and the survival of the nation. Because people believe that peace can be achieved by deliberate disarmament or that weapons technology can keep the nations permanently disarmed, they do not take steps to plan to fight war justly. Ramsey writes that such beliefs are based on wishful thinking and that steps toward just war must be taken now. He criticizes the public for ignoring "the difference between 25,000,000 dead as the probable result of all-out counterforce warfare and 215,000,000 dead as a result of all-out countercity warfare between the great powers."[10] He accuses them of turning away from any effort to make counterforce nuclear war, if it comes, fall far, far short of all-out nuclear war.

According to Ramsey, the just war theory should serve as the context for policy making. The United States should announce that as a matter of policy it will never be the first to use nuclear weapons—except tactical ones that may and will be used, against military force only, and not strategically against an enemy's heartland. Tactical nuclear weapons should be used against any invasion, even by conventional forces, and this US policy should be made clear to the Soviet Union. Tactical nuclear weapons will not be used for victory but for defense traditionally understood as protecting the border. If an invation force crosses the border, it will be attacked with tactical nuclear weapons.[11]

One of the great advantages of this policy, Ramsey says, is that it is credible and, therefore, more likely to deter aggression from a potential enemy. He believes that citizens are "morally obligated" to prepare for a just nuclear war.

Arguments Against Nuclear Weapons

Many Christians agree with these words of John Bennett: "If once our nation decided to use force, the justice of the cause would not cancel the moral horror in the use of nuclear weapons."[12]

In *Just and Unjust Wars: A Moral Argument With Historical Illustrations,* Michael Walzer looks critically at Paul Ramsey's ideas concerning just nuclear war. He believes that Ramsey, in extending the just war theory to apply to the use of nuclear weapons, has passed beyond what a just war can be. He writes that Ramsey's work "suggests the outer limits of the just war and the dangers of trying to extend those limits."[13]

One criticism that Walzer makes is that Ramsey's argument relies on the idea of acceptable, indirect death of innocents. Ramsey expects to kill people without aiming at them. "That may be a matter of some moral significance, but it does not seem significant enough to serve as the cornerstone of a justified deterrent."[14]

Walzer points out that the mere possession of nuclear weapons constitutes an implicit threat. If government policies claimed that, in keeping with Ramsey's desires, nuclear weapons will be used only against strategic forces, the weapons might still be used against population centers during a time of war. He counters Ramsey that the bomb is different from a sword or a rifle which may or may not be used against innocent people. It is designed as a weapon of mass destruction, and its deterrent value depends upon that fact (whether the killing is direct or indirect). The bomb serves the purpose of preventing war only by virtue of the implicit threat it poses. Walzer believes that all of Ramsey's nuclear policies rest ultimately on immoral

Despite our political persuasion,
prayer is still our highest
common denominator!

— FRIAR TUCK

threats.[15]

Others have also criticised Ramsey for wanting to make nuclear war fit the criteria of the just war. In *An Alternative to War*, Gordon Zahn compares justification of nuclear war to the fascist justification of genocide, the intentional burning of 200,000 people.[16] Though Ramsey claims that to be just, a nuclear war can and must be limited, others point out that there is no inherent limit to the measure of destruction and ruin that a nuclear war might bring.

At times, even military leaders have spoken out concerning the justification of nuclear war. General Douglas MacArthur said: "We must finally come to realize that war is outmoded as an instrument of political policy, that it provides no solution for international suicide. You cannot control war; you can only abolish it."[17]

The just war ethic has not outlived its usefulness. It is not that in this age of mass destruction weaponry the conditions for just war no longer apply. Rather, it is the just war criteria themselves that furnish the test (for both pacifists and nonpacifists) by which nuclear weapons are declared morally unacceptable. Major General Kermit Johnson puts it this way:

> There are many that have said that nuclear weapons have made the just war theory obsolete, but to me that's like saying that sin has made the Ten Commandments obsolete. . . . If indeed the criteria of the just war has been shattered by the characteristics of nuclear weapons and nuclear war, it does not make those criteria invalid but rather establishes them.[18]

Nuclear weapons have introduced a qualitatively new reality. In this nuclear era, just war theorists and Christian pacifists may be able to overcome their differences and reach a new consensus on the practical level. The two traditions may converge in the sense that both reject nuclear deterrence as a moral option.

Nuclear Pacifism

Just war theorists and biblical pacifists agree that the present realities of the nuclear age have brought with them a qualitatively new potential for both murderous violence and profound injustice. When applying the just war criteria to the nuclear war era, most conclude that there can be no just nuclear deterrence. Thus, both pacifists and just war adherents may consider themselves "nuclear pacifists." The just war advocates still believe that some uses of deadly force may be legitimate in some cases, but they can agree with the pacifists that nuclear weapons may never be justifiably used.

Larry Rasmussen of Union Theological Seminary in New York, states:

> It is not that just warriors have suddenly been converted to the pacifist version of the jointly-held norm (unexceptional nonviolence as a way of life) nor that the theological orientations no longer matter, or differ. Rather, the prudential judgments of just warriors have converged with the judgments of pacifists in those cases where lethal violence could take the feared shape of the mushroom firecloud.[19]

Nuclear pacifism (or even relative Christian pacifism) is quite different from pacifism of the historic peace church tradition. Nuclear pacifists do not assert that all war is sin or intrinsically evil, simply because it uses violence and does not abide by the Christian law of love as described in the Sermon on the Mount. However, nuclear pacifists do believe that war, with the development of nuclear weapons, has now become an evil that may no longer be justified. There simply is no way to morally condone the potential destructive power of nuclear weapons. Nuclear pacifists may have supported the just war theory in the past. When this idea is applied to nuclear war, however, it seems evident that such a war could never meet the just war criteria.

The earliest firm landmark in the development of nuclear pacifism from a faith perspective was a study done by the World Council of Churches in 1954. Here is part of their conclusion about the use of nuclear weapons:

> Although there are differences of opinion on many points, we are agreed on one point. This is that Christians should openly declare that the all-out use of these weapons should never be resorted to. Moreover, that Christians must oppose all policies which give evidence of leading to all-out war. Finally, if all-out war should occur, Christians should urge a cease fire, if necessary, on the enemy's terms, and resort to nonviolent resistance.[20]

Nuclear pacifists have developed several basic arguments against the use of nuclear weapons. Here is a summary:

> Nuclear weapons eliminate all distinction between combatants and noncombatants—their very nature is to be used against noncombatants.
> These weapons destroy all connection between war and justice.
> Threats are effective only if one is prepared to carry them out so it is immoral even to threaten to use nuclear weapons.
> These new weapons are designed to take the enemy by

surprise and to annihilate the enemy rather than to conclude a just peace with the enemy.

Nuclear weapons turn us all into murderers in our mentality—for that is the only mentality which can produce and use such weapons.

If the Church were to participate in an atomic war of annihilation it would destroy itself spiritually, even more than externally.

The harm nuclear weapons would cause is disproportionate to any good attainable by their use.

As Christians conscientiously pray about and study the nuclear weapons issue, one suspects that the number of nuclear pacifists will continue to grow.

7

Nuclear Deterrence

The moment has come . . . to look more deeply into the most basic premises underlying all nuclear weapons and to expose their unwisdom. That means a fresh and comprehensive critique of the dominant strategic idea of the post-World War II decades: nuclear deterrence.[1]

Christians are beginning to take a more critical look at US nuclear deterrence policy. They are asking questions that will be addressed in this chapter: What is nuclear deterrence? How does fear play a major role in nuclear deterrence? Can a nuclear war remain limited? Should we develop the "star wars" technology and defense system? How does the nuclear arms race affect the US economy?

Defining Nuclear Deterrence

To "deter" literally means to frighten or to strike terror. Deterrence means "dissuasion of a potential adversary from initiating an attack or conflict, often by the threat of unacceptable retaliatory damage."[2]

There are several ways of viewing nuclear deterrence. Alan Geyer, executive director of the Churches' Center for Theology and Public Policy and author of many peace-related articles and books, points out the following seven Christian positions or attitudes toward nuclear war:

1. Traditional pacifism — it is always morally wrong to commit lethal violence, regardless of the circumstances;
2. Nuclear pacifism — not all wars but all *nuclear* wars would be morally wrong;
3. Deterrence but non use — because of necessity we must have nuclear weapons as a deterrent, but it would be immoral for us to ever actually deploy the weapons;
4. Deterrence, but not for a first strike — it is moral to have nuclear weapons and even to use them in

some circumstances as long as we do not use them first;

5. First use option position—deterrence is a necessary doctrine in an evil world. We need to maintain the option to use nuclear weapons first in response to a conventional attack;

6. Counterforce approach—we should aim nuclear weapons at prime military targets rather than at civilians and cities, and then we must keep the nuclear exchange from escalating into an all-out nuclear war;

7. Preemptive strike—we should develop a nuclear defense policy (e.g., star wars technology) so that we can block a nuclear attack.[3]

Of the various positions listed above, pacifism and nuclear pacifism are the only ones that do not ultimately put their trust in nuclear weapons for protection. All of the other positions, though they differ in their approach and severity, argue that the US must rely on nuclear weapons. Some nuclear pacifists hold more than one of these positions. They agree with the second position that all nuclear wars would be morally wrong, and perhaps with positions three and seven.

After much study and testimony from experts with many of the above positions, the Catholic bishops wrote an important and well-publicized pastoral letter on war and peace: *The Challenge of Peace: God's Promise and Our Response* (1983). By and large they supported position three, although the bishops did not label it as such. They concluded that the possession of nuclear arms is permissible if deterrence moves into mutual arms reduction and *if* the weapons are never used under any circumstances. They also said that in the long run nuclear deterrence must be rejected. "Deterrence is not an adequate strategy as a long-term basis for peace; it is a transitional strategy justifiable only in conjunction with resolute determination to pursue arms control and disarmament."[4] The document quotes Pope John XXIII:

The fundamental principle on which our present peace depends must be replaced by another, which declares that the true and solid peace of nations consists not in equality of arms but in mutual trust alone.[5]

Geyer has described what he terms "the three nuclear ages."[6] He divides the post-Hiroshima years into three periods of contrasting disarmament trends. The first nuclear age (1945-1960) was a time of little seriousness about disarmament. The US was convinced of the advantages of nuclear monopoly and nuclear superiority, and it was too complacent about its technological genius to submit to any honest-to-goodness controls. On the other hand, the Soviet Union, paranoid about western threats to its own security, promoted propaganda for disarmament while building up its own strategic arsenals.

During the second nuclear age (1960-1974), there was a new sobriety about the arms race and the imminence of parity, or equality, with the Soviets. Although nuclear arsenals continued to multiply, this period marked the first serious efforts at negotiated disarmament and it produced numerous treaties and an era of détente, a relaxing of tensions.

The third nuclear age (1974-?) is marked by a many-faceted new nuclear crisis that came after a brief period in which the world had become increasingly complacent about the nuclear issues. This period involves basic issues of energy, economics, environment, health, international trade, international law enforcement, and others. It looks for a coherent nuclear policy which can cope with these many interconnected pressures.

Mutual Assured Destruction (MAD) is a US military deterrent policy that was foreseen by Winston Churchill in 1955. He said that by a process of sublime irony, survival will be the twin brother of annihilation.[7] This policy is based on the assumption that a potential aggressor will not attack the US if that nation knows that the US can and will respond with a massive nuclear attack on their nation. The ability to retaliate after an initial attack is known as second-strike capability. The idea is that no one will use nuclear weapons against the US because doing so would mean mutual suicide.

For the most part in the 1980s, the policy of MAD has been replaced or modified with the idea of counterforce. Geyer describes counterforce as the "unruly offspring of deterrence"[8] that increasingly is usurping the strategic authority deterrence has maintained for three decades.

Now, instead of trying to deter war, people are preparing to fight and "win" nuclear wars. "The 'unthinkable' has become most thinkable and calculable, and the concept of mutual destruction is crumbling fast."[9] The core concept of counterforce is a targeting doctrine. It suggests that rather than targeting cities, nuclear weapons should be aimed at military targets, such as bases, launchers, airports, and armament industries.

Counterforce is supported by some just war theorists who still believe that a war can remain limited. They believe that it fits the criteria of proportionality better than MAD. Counterforce advocates believe that armaments and technology are now sophisticated enough to allow more options than the "all or nothing" formula of massive retaliation. Unfortunately, counterforce makes nuclear war more likely to happen because it promotes the delusion that a limited nuclear war is possible.

Limited Nuclear War?

In their pastoral letter, the Catholic Bishops raise the issue of whether nuclear war can be contained:

> The issue of limited war is not simply the size of weapons contemplated or the strategies projected. The debate should include the psychological and political significance of crossing the boundary from the conventional to the nuclear arena in any form. To cross this divide is to enter a world where we have no experience of control, much testimony against its possibility, and therefore no moral justification for submitting the human community to this risk. We therefore express our view that the first imperative is to prevent any use of nuclear weapons and our hope that leaders will resist the notion that nuclear conflict can be limited, contained, or won in any traditional sense.[10]

Limited nuclear war was also one of the issues addressed by the Independent Commission On Disarmament and Security Issues, whose members came from many countries around the world. Their conclusions are found in *Common Security: A Blueprint for Survival* (1982). This report explained recent technological developments that have persuaded some people that nuclear wars could be limited and need not result in global destruction. Examples of such developments include improvement in the accuracy of long-range missiles, the development of nuclear weapons with relatively small explosive yields, and the availability of detailed and precise maps of potential targets derived from satelite intelligence systems. The US possesses the technological ability to attack military targets without targeting civilian cities.

However, the Commission report concluded that military analysts are in error to claim that conflicts involving the use of nuclear weapons, both on the battlefield and against targets, could remain limited.[11] Many reasons are given to explain why military strategists should not expect a "controlled" nuclear exchange. The malfunctions which have plagued the space programs of several countries are a microcosm of the sort of problem that could have a profound impact on the course of any nuclear exchange. In an actual nuclear exchange, there will almost certainly exist what has been termed "the fog of war":

> the combination of uncertainty, misinformation, physical pressures, and psychological stress that accompanies any combat operation . . . The underlying dynamic would almost inevitably propel the conflict into larger and larger proportions.[12]

Ambassador James Wadsworth commented on the assumption that a nuclear war can remain limited if only military targets are attacked, as the counterforce model proposes. He explained:

> Even if war should begin as a counterforce war it would quickly expand into a war against cities and people. Because many cities are close to missile bases and airfields, it has been estimated that some thirty million Americans would be killed in a first counterforce-type strike. The first bombs to fall would knock out most communications and reconnaissance facilities. Neither government could know whether the other was "playing the game," which forces were still in existence, and what its own men were doing. In such confusion, total war would be almost inescapable.[13]

Military officials do not agree on the extent to which a

nuclear exchange could be limited. The US Department of Defense and the administration acknowledge that use of strategic nuclear weapons by one superpower against the other can be expected to escalate.

Many defense authorities who realize the impossibility of a limited nuclear war are turning to a "Strategic Defense Initiative" system popularly called "Star Wars." They hope Star Wars technology will solve nuclear defense problems by shooting down incoming missiles in space. Unfortunately, space weaponry only compounds the problems and increases the arms race.

You have heard it said "an eye for an eye and a tooth for a tooth" but I say, if anyone strikes you on the right cheek turn the other also † Love your enemies and pray for those who persecute you † Judge not, that you be not judged † Why do you see the speck in another's eye but do not notice the log in your own? If your neighbor has something against you, leave your gift at the altar and go, make your peace † All who take the sword shall perish by the sword † Blessed are the peacemakers, for they shall be called children of God † Have salt in yourselves and be at peace with one another † Would that even today you knew the things that make for peace! † But now they are hid from your eyes † In me you may have peace. In the world you have tribulation; but be of good cheer, I have overcome the world † Peace I leave with you, my peace I give to you, not as the world gives do I give to you.

Star Wars Technology

The Star Wars program was proposed in March 1983. It is a program which involves laser technology and the deployment of a space-based missile defense system. The ultimate goal of this system is to create a "shield" which would destroy an attack by enemy missiles and warheads. In theory, such a defensive shield would keep the Soviet Union from launching a nuclear first strike against the United States. Advocates of the system warn that without such a defensive shield the Soviets might be tempted to launch a first strike in the belief that we could be damaged sufficiently for them to "win' a nuclear exchange It is also argued that this system could make nuclear missile weapons obsolete because these weapons could be destroyed by non-nuclear (laser) weapons. This type of "perfect defense" would mean the end of nuclear ballistic weapons systems.

The quest for strategic defense started decades ago. During the 1970s the US and the USSR decided that such systems were too unworkable and costly to pursue in a serious way. Both countries realized that space weapons could ultimately be ineffective, which was part of the reasoning behind the Anti ballistic Missile Treaty of 1972. President Nixon and Secretary Brezhnev signed the ABM Treaty under the SALT I (Strategic Arms Limitation Talks) agreement, and many experts consider the ABM Treaty as "the most significant arms control treaty signed to date."[14]

A serious problem with the Reagan Star Wars proposal is that the cost of the missile system is astounding. According to a *New York Times* article in 1985,[15] Star Wars is envisioned as a $26 billion research program which is more than was spent in research for the Manhattan Project *and* the Apollo moon program. The total cost to develop and deploy the system has been estimated to be at least 800 billion dollars (or $1000 billion according to former Secretary of Defense, James Schlesinger). In order to better comprehend the amount of money that is being proposed, consider this comparison. If someone received one million dollars a day, every day since the time Christ was born, that person would still only have 700 billion dollars; not enough for research, manufacture, and deployment of the missile defense system.

Consider too, that it is not possible for such a missile defense system to be completely effective. It would be susceptible to countermeasures, for example: it could not shield against attacks by the Soviet Union's low flying cruise missiles, by their long-range bombers, or by short-range submarine-launched weapons. In addition, the space-based components of the defense would themselves be vulnerable to attack.

A system could not be built that would be 100 percent effective and 99 percent is not good enough. If 1,000 missiles were launched and only 1 percent got through, those remaining 10 missiles could do enough damage to destroy the US.

Space weaponry could also be destabilizing if the

Soviet Union believes we really can develop the SDI system. Their ability to counter an attack from us is threatened. If we could develop a defensive shield against their weapons, we could then launch an offensive attack against them without fear of retaliation. The Soviets would feel left open to an attack from us and unable to strike back. In order to avoid being placed in a "defenseless" position against us, the Soviets might go to dangerous measures to keep the US from completing Star Wars. Even though Americans feel sure that the US would not initiate a first strike against the Soviet Union, the Soviets are as afraid of us as we are of them. It makes sense for them to view Star Wars as a potentially offensive system.

More and more experts who have worked on aspects of SDI are beginning to admit that building such a system would not make the US more secure. For example, Robert Bowman, who is president of the Institute for Space and Security Studies, former vice president of Space Communications Company, and past Director of the Air Force Space Division, recently wrote *Star Wars: Defense or Death Star?*[16] In this thoughtful book he explains why SDI would not improve national security. He states that none of the proposed types of Star Wars technology would protect us. In fact, there would be an *increase* in the likelihood of a nuclear war with the USSR because the Star Wars defense requires anti-satellite (ASAT) weapons. There is a much greater chance of accidental war with ASAT weapons. Bowman recommends that the US join the Soviet moratorium on the testing of ASAT weapons and on the deployment of any weapon in space. He calls for scientists from both countries to join with others from around the world for a discussion of space technology which can be used to provide global security rather than triggering a nuclear holocaust. He concludes:

> We can use space to enrich life—or to end it. Together, we can prevail in the hostile environment of space and, as a planetary people, use the knowledge and riches it can provide to better life on earth—or we can export our instruments of death beyond the planet entrusted to us by God and thereby loose forces which could bring about its destruction. Let us choose wisely. Let us choose life.[17]

Nuclear Deterrence and Fear

Alan Geyer has written that deterrence is rooted in the common and legitimate human experience of fear in the face of serious dangers. Deterrence occurs when those dangers are so serious that they discourage a contemplated course of action. "Deterrence is the manipulation of fear. It is the deliberate promotion of fear as a weapon of dissuasion."[18] Deterrence is based on the ultimate irrationality: it relies on the common sense, rationality, and humanity of those whom we consider our "enemies" and thus distrust the most.

Fear has played an important role in the arms race. When one side makes its weapons more destructive, accurate, evasive, and mobile, the other side fears that it is lagging behind and begins a build-up of weapons. Each nation fears that its ability to retaliate might be made ineffective by the enemy's superiority. History demonstrates the flaw in the bigger and better bombs argument: every time a new generation of US weapons is built, the Russians match us. New weapons are increasingly difficult to verify, and each side thinks that it has even more reason to fear. As fear mounts, the nation's military leaders become paranoid and irrational.

An interesting model has been used to justify the necessity of war and the need for a strong nuclear defense. The question is asked, "Wouldn't you do anything possible to prevent a criminal who has broken into your home from killing your loved ones?" Ultimately, many Americans fear that the Russians or some other "enemy" will, in essence, "break into our home (land)" and destroy us. Because of this fear, we are willing to spend our time, energy, resources, and trillions of dollars on an arms race that could end in either an accidental or a planned nuclear war.

Dale Aukerman, author of *Darkening Valley: A Biblical Perspective on Nuclear War,* explains that the model of the family under attack is not really an accurate model for the situation between the US and the USSR. He gives a more accurate analogy:

> You and your family are at one end of a long large room. An opponent and his family are at the other end. Earlier you each had a gun leveled at the other and the other's family.

But then you both realized that your opponent might be able to shoot fast enough to prevent return fire. You each, with help from the family, frantically proceeded to set up across each end of the room an ever-increasing array of shotguns, rifles, and machine guns, all interconnected, primed for firing also at the pull of triggering wires (which would be tripped even by riddled bodies toppling over) and aimed partly at the weaponry, partly at the people in the other end of the room.

As you each work away at the ingenious buildup of firearms, you shout warnings toward the other end of the room. There are times of heightened tension when each thinks that the other may be at the point of firing first in hope of coming through at least somewhat better that way than if he were fired upon first. There is the constant danger that some gun may go off by accident, that a triggering wire may be pulled unintentionally, or even that an intruder may burst in. The two of you have shouted to each other across the length of the room about the possibility of a partial or total dismantling of the two countering weaponry setups; but neither of you sees any feasible way this could be done. So each of you keeps adding the leveled guns and the triggering wires across his end of the room because the other must be prevented from concluding that he might be able to fire first and get away with it.[19]

The nuclear arms race is fueled by the fear that an "enemy" will get ahead and attack as well as the fear of economic failure if armaments and military-based jobs were lost.

The Nuclear Arms Race and the Economy

Economic practices are certainly involved in decisions that are made concerning nuclear deterrence. According to Robert Aldridge, author of *The Counterforce Syndrome,* the drive for profits by large weapons producers increases the arms race. Aldridge was an engineer at Lockheed, the nation's number one arms producer, for sixteen years.

Aldridge explained that military prime contracting exceeds $42 billion annually. Large corporations constantly lobby the Congress and the Pentagon. Many of the top defense officials come from industry and they have an industrial viewpoint. Those backgrounds and personal interests make unbiased decisions difficult, yet these same weapons contractors decide differently when business opportunities appear in other areas. For instance, some contractors sought export licenses in order to sell passenger jets to the Soviet Union. "The pattern seems to be that the Soviet threat surges when there is a need to drum up support for weapons contracts, but shrinks as opportunities to market US goods in Russia present themselves."[20]

Aldridge points out that fear of losing jobs is an obstacle to disarmament. Many senators and representatives feel trapped — they want to use some military funds to meet human and social needs, but they also fear the possibility of losing jobs for constituents back home if military appropriations are cut. However, an analysis of employment data suggests that weapons programs do not necessarily provide employment.[21]

A pamphlet by Covenant for Peace explains that the myth that defense spending creates more jobs has been proved false. Actually, military spending creates relatively few jobs because it is highly automated and capital-intensive. For example, the same one billion dollars which creates 14,400 jobs in military radio and communications equipment, could be used to create 44,500 jobs in educational services. Military spending also adds to inflation because it generates dollars for arms contractors but adds nothing productive to our economy. It increases the price of scarce materials and resources, and it is riddled with waste and cost overruns.[22]

The Independent Commission on Disarmament and Security Issues addressed the problem that military spending creates for the economy. They suggest that expenditure on nuclear weapons is a form of consumption requiring resources that could otherwise have been used in civilian society. They provide important comparative statistics such as, "the price of one nuclear submarine with its missiles would provide a hundred thousand working years of nursing care for old people."[23] Their report states that the sacrifice of human, material, and technological resources required by military spending is likely to be particularly costly for rich countries as well as for poor countries. They conclude that if increased military spending is continued then poverty, unemployment, inflation, and the threat of world recession will become much worse.

For pacifists and most just war theorists, nuclear deterrence raises many moral and strategical problems. It is not an adequate solution to our need for security. Alan Geyer summarizes this issue:

> Ultimately, the issue is not what kinds of nuclear weapons we need nor how many of them: it is how best to overcome the demonic myth that our security requires nuclear arms at all ... the very dominance of deterrence among American Christians for three decades points to the lact of alternative theologies of war-avoidance. The fact of the matter is not that deterrence has triumphed over strong and worthy opponents; it is that few Christian thinkers have ever thought very hard or systematically about how to avoid war - except through the manipulation of terror or the fabrication of international machinery. [24]

As Geyer noted, few Christian thinkers have thought about alternatives to nuclear deterrence; few have thought about how to avoid war without manipulation of terror or the use of weapons of destruction. Yet more and more Christians looking at the arms race are saying, "This has got to stop!" Some creative ideas are being discussed by nuclear pacifists and other persons interested in peace as they search for solutions to the nuclear arms race.

8

Alternatives to the Nuclear Arms Race

I dream of giving birth to a child who will ask, "Mother, what was war?"

People should look at all of their alternatives before making any major decision. In trying to find a way to defend themselves, we have all too often assumed that violence and weapons of mass destruction are the only answers. Millions of people feel that nuclear arms must be relied upon even though they may be considered an "immoral necessity."

Fortunately, not everyone sees nuclear weapons as a necessity. They feel that we can and must protect ourselves in other ways. New strategies and techniques are being discussed and developed. These non-nuclear alternatives are far from foolproof at this point, and may take years before they can be fully practiced. These alternatives have much to offer and challenge us to come up with even better strategies for defense. Perhaps bits and pieces of various alternative ideas can be combined and used to develop a defense that no longer has to rely on nuclear weapons. This chapter describes some of the many ideas being discussed as alternatives to the nuclear arms race.

Groups Discovering Alternatives

The Nuclear Weapons Freeze movement itself does not emphasize specific alternatives to dependence on nuclear weapons. However, it calls us to halt the arms race as a first step toward nuclear disarmament. It asks for an immediate, mutual, and verifiable freeze on the testing, production, and deployment of nuclear weapons and to negotiate reductions in nuclear arms. It argues that the building of new missiles which threaten to permanently destabilize the US/USSR balance and which make effective arms control more difficult must be stopped. At present,

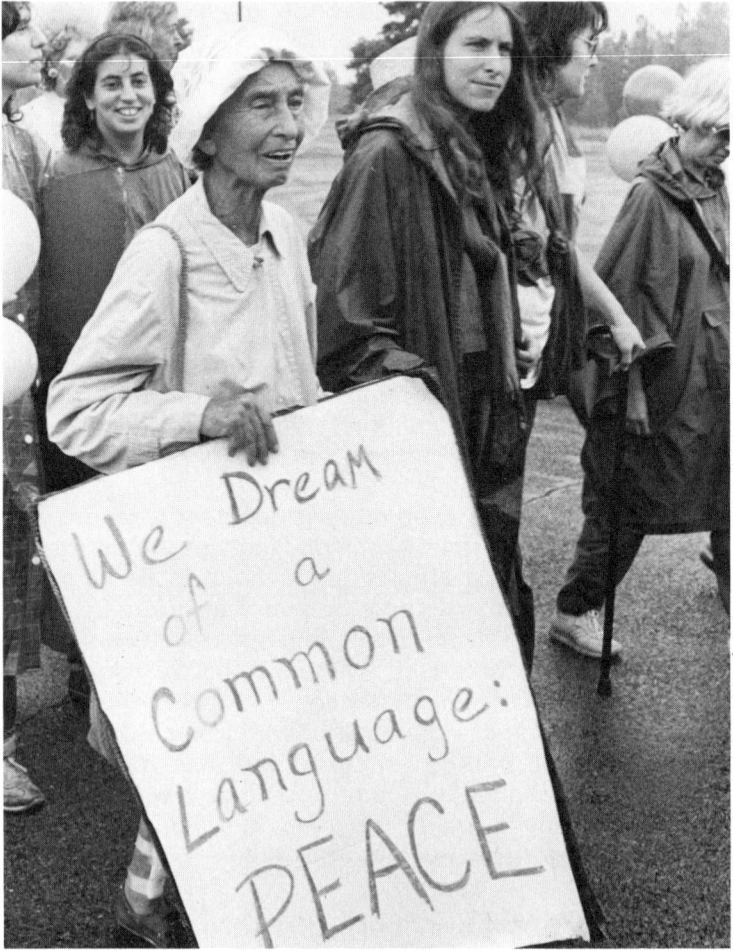

August 1, 1983. Marching from Sampson State Park, Women's Peace Encampment, August 1, 1983. Photo by Nancy Clover © 1983.

nuclear arms treaties are verified by spy satellites, radar, and other electrical devices operated independently by each country. A freeze must occur soon before weapons are built that are more and more difficult to verify. The freeze movement is a grass roots movement supported by Republicans and Democrats, business leaders and labor, a wide spectrum of religious leaders, people of all races and all economic lebels, and persons from all parts of the country.

Universities are becoming more involved in finding alternatives to the nuclear arms race. *The Center for International Affars* at Harvard University has started a new program on "Nonviolent Sanctions in Conflict and Defense." The program conducts research and policy studies. Its objective is to determine the degree to which nonviolent sanctions may provide effective substitutes for violent options in resolving problems of dictatorship, war, genocide, and oppression.[2] Another example is *The Center for Conflict Resolution* at George Mason University in Virginia which seeks to promote ideas for creative resolution of conflicts. It provides a master of science degree program in conflict management. This program trains students in new and increasingly precise methods of conflict problem solving. Problem solving displaces confrontation and adversarism, fighting and war as methods for dealing with group and personal quarrels and disputes.[3]

INTERHELP is an international network based on the conviction that peace, justice, and a healthy planet demand more than politics alone. It emphasizes the importance of dealing with people's heart and spirit — their feelings, visions, and deepest inner responses to the world. It trains people to lead innovative workshops and other programs that integrate the emotional and the political, the personal and the planetary. For example, some workshops move participants through three stages: imaging, scenario writing, and action planning. At each stage group members are invited to release imaginative energies in order to "invent" a desired future, one consonant with their most deeply held values and beliefs. As a result of this approach, new possibilities are conceived, and new images of strategies become possible. After people gain clear images of the future society they wish to work toward, a course of action to contribute to its formation is discussed.[4]

New and exciting ideas are being discussed in the area of parenting for peace, and groups such as *Educators for Social Responsibility (ESR)* are helping children to deal with their fears about nuclear war. Many children believe that there is going to be a nuclear war during their lifetime and that they will not survive it. Parents and educators must give children a sense of hope and responsibility for the future. In one of the many programs started by ESR , beginners learn to resolve playground conflicts or to share toys without fighting. As they grow older, they read books, such as John Hersey's *Hiroshima,* learn to define kilotons, study the effect of nuclear blasts and radiation, and stage mock classroom "wars" between the superpowers.[5]

The Albert Einstein Institution was founded in 1984 as a tax-exempt, public foundation to support the research and implementation of nonviolence by individuals and groups such as those mentioned above. It is committed to the exploration of the nonviolent alternatives to the use of violence in politics. Its work focuses on two parallel objectives: to promote basic research and to develop a public affairs program that will communicate effectively with policy makers, scholars, and the general public. The Institution points out that, contrary to what we have been taught, there have been significant successes with nonviolent strategies. It reminds us that the independence movement in India, the civil rights movement in the United States, the recent opposition movement in Poland, and scores of similar struggles have shown remarkable results. The Institution is named after Albert Einstein because he was deeply concerned with the problems of war, dictatorship, genocide, and social oppression, and because he was willing to accept change and to explore new approaches.

MICHIGAN CHRISTIAN ADVOCATE

Our Creed...

"We're just those strange birds who believe that peacemakers are ultimately stronger than peacekeepers!"

Bowman's Steps to Peace[6]

Robert Bowman, as previously mentioned, is author of *Star Wars: Defense or Death Star?* He believes that the Americans and Soviets can work together on mutual interests and can even become allies. He does not believe naively that this can happen overnight, but recommends several gradual steps that both nations should take.

According to Bowman, there is no quick technological fix to the problem of defending ourselves from the Russians. It may not be easy, but the surest way of getting rid of an enemy is to make them a friend. The US and the USSR forged a temporary "friendship of convenience" during World War II because there was a common enemy. With smaller steps, a more lasting relationship could be built. Following are some of the steps that Bowman suggests.

First, a war in the short run should be avoided by maintaining the current deterrent posture. Government and military leaders should be encouraged to stop downgrading deterrent measures with scare tactics in order to justify increases in military budgets. The US is not now, nor has it ever been, "number two" strategically with the USSR. The respect that other nations have for our military power will only be lessened by this approach.

Second, both sides need to recognize a mutual vulnerability, the mutual impotence of nuclear forces for anything but deterrence, and a mutual interest in survival.

Once the common problem is recognized, actions can be taken which reduce the need or temptation to strike first. This comes when either side feels that their forfces are vulnerable. The fear is that weapons must be used in order not to be lost. Advanced technology, such as MIRVs (multiple independently targeted reentry vehicles), increases vulnerability and thus increases the danger. The Star Wars systems would create a new front line of totally vulnerable forces and would hinder early warning systems of other nations. To increase stability, early warning systems need to be improved, warheads limited, and a nuclear freeze implemented to stop the building of more and more accurate delivery systems which are, thus, first strike weapons.

After a stable balance of nuclear weapons is achieved and its continuation guaranteed through some sort of freeze, the threat that each side poses can be reduced. A careful, balanced reduction in offensive and vulnerable weapons could begin the process. The "build-down" theory proposed by the Reagan administration would decrease stability by replacing many unsophisticated retaliatory weapons with a few highly accurate first-strike weapons on each side. However, the "threat-reduction" step, as proposed by Bowman, would keep stability in the forefront as weapons are slowly bargained away.

The superpowers could then begin the process of providing systems for ensuring common security once a stable balance is reached. For example, a peace monitoring system could be built which would consist of an international earth-observation satellite system to provide military intelligence about all nations to all nations. All countries would receive information about potential threats to their sovereignty in order to deter agression. A restructured and reinvigorated United Nations might be able to use such a system to aid in its peacekeeping role.

The resources now spent on military weapons could be used gradually to solve other problems such as world hunger. These resources include the world's spending on the military a trillion dollars a year, technology, and brainpower. Many of the world's scientists and engineers are working on means of destruction; these talented scientists could be freed to work on improved health care, better sources of renewable energy, and cleaning up air and water pollution.

Eventually, the nations of the world will need to establish effective and respected international laws which will allow disputes between nations to be solved peaceably. Much of the machinery for this already exists in the United Nations charter, treaties between countries, and the World Court. However, this body of international law will remain largely ineffective until the superpowers subject themselves to it—even when they disagree with it. In addition, world peace through law can succeed only if the demands of international justice are satisfied.

Bowman believes that if steps such as these are followed, then the US will, in time, be able to cooperate and ally with the Soviets. "To follow the path outlined above will require courageous leadership on both sides. If the attempt is made, however, it is bound to succeed."[7]

Civilian-Based Defense

Civilian-based defense (CBD), a part of the concept of "transarmament," is a planned nonviolent defense strategy based upon action by nonmilitary citizens. It attempts to defeat military aggression by using the resistance of the civilian population to make it impossible for the invader or usurper to establish and maintain control over the invaded nation.[8]

Transarmament is the change from one defense system to a fundamentally different one, for example, from military to nonmilitary defense. Such a change does not leave a country defenseless, however. Transarmament incorporates the idea that a nation accustomed to defense by military means might choose to use nonviolent, civilian struggle rather than military weapons to preserve the society's freedom, sovereignty and constitutional systems.[9]

The chart, "Defense Strategies: How They Differ," illustrates how civilian-based defense differs from military defense.

The following passage from Gene Sharp's booklet, *Making the Abolition of War a Realistic Goal,* provides some details on how CBD would work:

> Various population groups and institutions would have responsibility for particular defense tasks, depending on the exact issues at stake. For example . . . journalists and editors, refusing to submit to censorship would publish newspapers illegally in large editions or many small editions — as happened in the Russian 1905 Revolution and in several Nazi-occupied countries. Free radio programs would continue from hidden transmitters — as happened in Czechoslovakia in 1968. Clergymen would preach the duty to refuse help to the invader — as happened in the Netherlands under the Nazis. Politicians, civil servants, judges, and the like by ignoring or defying the enemy's illegal orders, would keep the normal machinery of government, the courts, etc. out of his control — as happened in the German resistance to the Kapp Putsch in 1920 . . . Teachers would refuse to introduce propaganda into the schools — as happened in Norway under the Nazis . . . Workers and managers would impede exploitation of the country by selective strikes, delays, and obstructionism — as happened in the Ruhr in 1923 . . . These defense tasks are only il-

lustrative of a multitude of specific forms of defense action which would be possible.[10]

The idea of CBD did not originate with Gene Sharp, Gandhi began writing about the possibilities of national defense by nonviolent resistance in 1931. Soon others suggested nonviolent resistance as a "substitute for war." By 1958 a civilian-based defense concept reached a new level of interest and politicians and the military became involved as never before.

Defense Strategies: How They Differ

Point of Comparison	Military Strategy	Civilian-Based Strategy
The work of resisting aggression is done . . .	on behalf of the population.	by the population.
Defense leadership is . . .	stationed at military bases.	in residence, in the town and cities to be defended.
Defensive strength is centered in . . .	nuclear and conventional weapons/armed forces.	a unified population, prepared in advance to resist agression nonviolently.
Aggression is deterred by . . .	The certitude of mutual destruction.	the certitude that benefits to be derived from aggression will be minimized and the indirect costs will be maximized.
The power of the enemy is countered by . . .	violent pre-emptive strike or violent retaliation.	nation-wide noncooperation and active nonviolent resistance, combined with political and economic sanctions applied by all.

Defense *planning*...	requires highly skilled personnel/ lower-level personnel are expected to obey/civil liberties sometimes narrowed or curtailed for sake of national security.	is done largely at the local level, within guide lines set at higher level/ democratic processes are preserved and encouraged.
If aggression against the territory of the US were attempted . . .	countless deaths and injuries would result. Destruction of property and the environment would be virtually certain. Chaotic conditions certain because of disruption of all internal systems.	the cities, the environment and most internal systems would remain intact. People could devote all their energies to repulsing the aggressors.

CBD as an alternative to nuclear defense began to be taken more seriously in the 1960s when literature such as Quincy Wright's anthology, *Preventing World War III: Some Proposals* appeared. Since the mid-1960s, after Gene Sharp began to discuss the need for a functional substitute for war, the movement and theory for CBD has grown considerably. Various governments have become interested, and major academic conferences on the concept have been held in Finland, Sweden, Belgium, Norway, and the US.

CBD has the potential to protect the American way of life within our country, but it cannot protect the "American way of life" abroad or US economic interests in the developing countries. The US has a commitment to NATO allies in Europe that cannot be met with CBD, but some European countries, such as Denmark, the Netherlands, Norway, Sweden, and Switzerland, have pieces of CBD as part of their defense strategy that could be operative within a decade. As allies of the US become more able to protect themselves with CBD, the burden it carries for the defense of others could be lifted. This, in turn, would free the US to reexamine its own defense needs.[12]

With a CBD strategy our military institutions would begin to change. The need for a Defense Department would still be present but civilian struggle would replace military defense which relied on increasingly sophisticated weaponry and technolgy. Although there would be civilian casualties, projections are that they would be much fewer than in military conflict. There are many examples of effective CBD, although it is usually not labeled as such. Examples include the US civil rights movement, Norway's resistance to German domination during World War II, and India's struggle for independence from Great Britain.[13]

Some people consider nonviolent resistance such as CBD one of the great discoveries of the twentieth century:

> Like the atom, it has existed since the dawn of creation, but we are just beginning to discover its power. The fierce energy of unseen atomic nuclei has been unleashed to create a weapons system of limited destructiveness. It is possible as well that the unseen psychological force capability of nonviolent resistance has the potential, once harnessed, to create a weapons system of extraordinary magnitude. Nonviolent resistance may be a way to wage "war without violence."[14]

Turning Enemies into Allies

One of the most difficult things that Jesus Christ calls his followers to do is to love our enemies. Yet when we do, it is one of the most beautiful, life-changing, freeing experiences. We are released from our hatred, our anger, our desire to seek revenge. Being human, we know that we cannot forgive and love our enemies if we try to do it with our own strength alone. Only through prayer and asking God to help us can we slowly grow to accept and understand those with whom we disagree. In time, if we are open to God's healing love, we can grow to love our enemies.

Throughout history, nation states have considered some countries their enemies and others as allies. The irony is that, over a period of time, enemies can become allies and vice versa. This has been true throughout much of European history. An obvious example is the US and USSR who were allies against Nazi Germany, and currently the US and West Germany who are allies against the Soviet

Union. We do not fear the nuclear missiles of European allies. A nuclear attack by the US, Great Britain, or France on one another is unthinkable. If the Soviets were allies, the build-up of massive piles of nuclear weapons to protect "us" from "them" would not be necessary. What a different world this would be!

Of course to many people, the idea of US-USSR cooperation seems naive, unrealistic, and utopian.

GOD'S LOVE ooo

CAN TURN "ALIENS" INTO FRIENDS!
—FRIAR TUCK.

However, even if it were, it challenges us to take a more critical look at the US/USSR relationship. Could not a bridge of mutuality be built between these two superpowers? Even though many Americans feel idealogical differences prevent the US and the USSR from becoming allies, certainly not friends, an improved relationship with the Soviets can be worked at. US and USSR citizens can try to understand one another.

John C. Bennet, author of many books and articles concerning peace in the nuclear era, writes that we must study the "enemy," find our way to new relations with them, and work towards mutual understanding. He points out that before there is a willingness to work on relationships with the Soviets, some changes will need to be made in our attitude toward them. For example, we must understand that they are at least as afraid of us as we are of them, and that they no longer believe in the possibility of victory in a nuclear war.[15]

Some exciting things at a non-governmental level are being done to build relationships with the Soviets which, obviously, cannot be built without interaction. Exchanging visits with them is an excellent way to start. Church groups are learning the importance of this and are sending representatives to help bridge the gap by talking with Christians in the USSR.

An example of one such trip is the "Journey of Reconciliation." Sponsored by the American Fellowship of Reconciliation and the Manchester College Peace Studies Institute (North Manchester, Indiana), forty-two North Americans traveled to the Soviet Union and Eastern Europe for three weeks. The group contacted religious groups and peace organizations with these goals:

> 1. to understnad the experience of persons and their attitudes toward the arms race and the possibilities for détente and disarmament;
> 2. to learn the role of churches in the USSR and Eastern Europe; and
> 3. to establish personal contacts with citizens of Soviet bloc nations which will develop into deeper understanding and further exchanges between citizens of the East and West.[16]

The Soviet government itself has sponsored international workcamps and conferences. People from around the world met for one such conference which discussed the value of student/work exchange programs in promoting greater understanding of global enviornmental and peace issues. They also planned sessions with the Soviet Peace Committee in preparation for their "1985 Youth Festival" in Moscow which had 15,000 participants from 92 nations.[17]

For those who cannot physically go to the Soviet Union or talk with a Soviet citizen personally, there are many written resources that can be read. The average Soviet citizen knows far more about the United States and its people than Americans know about the Soviet Union. A common perception that is taught both in American school and through the media is that Soviet people are evil, godless communists that want to take over the world. People hear this so often that they tend to believe it without questioning. Few schools offer courses on the Russian language, economy, history, or social structures. Because we know so little about the Russian people, it is easy for us to stereotype them and thus, dehumanize them. We need to make a commitment to serious study of the Russian people, their government, and their country.

Studying the Soviet Union and the Soviet people, sending groups to visit them, joining with them at workcamps, reading about their customs, language, economy, history, and social structures—these are all ways that we can start to turn "enemies" into allies.

Robert Bowman writes about the possibility of friendly relations with the Soviets:

> It was only a few years ago that China was a more feared enemy than the Soviet Union—and yet we now call China a "friend" . . . Germany and Japan were our mortal enemies (remember how we demonized them in the patriotic movies and posters of World War II?) Now they are our strongest allies. And, of course, our greatest historical enemy, the nation which actually invaded and bloodied American soil and burned our capitol—was Great Britain. Who dares to say that Soviet-American friendship is impossible![18]

Even before we reach the point at which our enemies can be considered allies, we need to work together with them in ways that wil lead to a common security.

Common Security

> In the modern age, security cannot be obtained unilaterally. Economically, politically, culturally, and—most important—militarily, we live in an increasingly interdependent world. The security of one nation cannot be bought at the expense of others. The danger of nuclear war alone assures the validity of this proposition. But the obvious economic and political inter-relationships between different nations and different parts of the world strongly reinforce the point . . . We face common dangers and thus must also promote our security in common.[19]

The above passage is from the Independent Commission on Disarmament and Security Issues report. The Commission came to the conclusion that no nation can achieve true security by itself; security in the nuclear age means mutual security and they named their report *Common Security: A Blueprint for Survival.* The Commission's members, consisting of representatives from sixteen countries, including the US and the USSR, agreed on a concrete program of action. Their recommendations constitute practical steps which could produce a genuine and significant improvement in the international political climate and real progress toward arms control and a reduced risk of nuclear war.[20]

The Commission proposes that a gradual political process be pursued in which world-wide common security is achieved. Cooperation must replace confrontation in resolving conflicts of interest. "Nations must come to understand that the maintenance of world peace must be given a higher priority than the assertion of their own ideological or political positions."[21]

There are several principles of common security which the Commission suggests that countries ought to adopt as the basis for their security policies. Examples of these principles are: all nations have a legitimate right to security; military force is not a legitimate instrument for resolving disputes between nations; security cannot be attained through military superiority, and reductions and qualitative limitations of armaments are necessary for the common security.[22]

The Commission makes recommendations which, when taken together, constitute a broad program for substantial progress towards arms limitation and disarmament. The recommendations fall into six categories: the nuclear challenge and East-West relations, assuring confidence among the states, curbing the qualitative arms competition, strengthening the US security system, regional approaches to security, and economic security. They conclude: "A doctrine of common security must replace the present expedient of deterrence through armaments. International peace must rest on a commitment to joint survival rather than a threat of mutual destruction."[23]

Even as American build nuclear weapons aimed at the Soviet Union, they ship the Soviets more food than has ever moved between two nations. Dorann Gunderson, a Republican legislator, expressed the irony of this situation: "It's not logical . . . We and the Soviets are like Siamese twins. We may have two heads and think differently, but our mutual self-interests are overwhelming.[24]

The United Nations

The Commission on Disarmament and Security Issues calls the international community to reexamine the United Nations and to enable it to play a stronger peacekeeping role, as was originally intended. There have been some creative ideas developed for ways in which the UN could be strengthened to help maintain peace. For example, Robert McCan, Associate for Research and Development at the Churches' Center for Theology and Public Policy in Washington, DC, has developed a program that could be operated by the UN.

McCan's comprehensive program for conflict resolution has eight points:

1. The UN should develop a code of ethics for relationships among nations.

2. Nations should live by international law and the UN should have some means of enforcing this law. Nations often break international law because it is not enforced.

3. An early warning system of conflict reporting should be developed.

4. A system of fact-finding, reporting, and conciliation should be established.

5. Establishing a commission on mediation and arbitration would help to settle differences and grievances peacefully rather than settling them in war.

6. The International Court of Justice, which presently cannot enforce its decisions, should be strengthened.

7. A UN police force (different from an army) should be established to deal with conflicts that were not successfully handled by mediation.

8. Agape (i.e., love) troops should be established by a non-governmental organization. These troops would be highly trained and paid a small salary. Their tasks would be to work for the human interests of both sides of a conflict, to be willing to be killed but not to kill, to try to keep war from breaking out or getting worse, and to develop sympathy for peace.[25] The Witness for Peace Program on the Nicaraguan border is not connected with the UN, but it is an example of one way agape troops could be effective.

The alternatives to the nuclear arms race addressed in this chapter are only a few of the many new and creative ideas being discussed by responsible church leaders and others. Looked at briefly here, each deserves further explanation and study. None of them has been perfectly developed. However, they provide a starting point from which to dream of improvements to these alternatives, or for creating new proposals. Ultimately, they give us hope—hope that nuclear weapons need not be considered an immoral necessity, and the hope that one day there will be peace.

9

Plans for Action

The word *shalom* occurs 300 times in the Old Testament. It represents peace and complete well-being for all creatures with God. It describes the oneness of creation, with everything on earth living under God in security, harmony, and joy.[2] Jesus can work through us to bring *shalom* to this world. We are all part of the body of Christ; we can be instruments of God's love and peace. Each of us can be messengers, proclaiming the promise of *shalom*.

This chapter will address specific action that Christians can take individually and with the faith community, guided through prayer. When our action is not based on prayer, it becomes fearful, fanatical, bitter, and more an expression of survival instincts than of faith in God as the God of the living. Prayer empowers us.

Action for Individuals

Activities as simple as telling a neighbor how one feels about the arms race is an important step in the right direction. Many opinions are formed largely in discussions with friends and relatives. Discussing the issues is a responsibility for all citizens in a democracy and US citizens are privileged to live in a country where they can voice and act on these opinions. It is important to use that voice to share feelings about issues such as war and peace.

Mail, phone calls, and telegrams can have an impact on public officials and the media. Writing one's congressional representatives is not as difficult as it seems at first, and it does make a difference. Only one out of every ten citizens ever writes a letter to a representative, senator, or the president. The others may feel that their letters won't make a difference; however, mail is very important to today's members of Congress because the issues are more complex and the sheer number of legislative bills is increasing. For example, Morris Udall, member of the House of Representatives from Arizona, said, "My mailbag is my best 'hot line' to the people back home. On several occasions a single, thoughtful, factually persuasive letter did change my mind. . . ."[3]

An easy way to keep in touch with our representatives is to keep a stack of postcards ready and jot down opinions whenever an item in the news seems important. It is particularly helpful to send these postcards or letters while the issue is being debated in committee or before a key vote. The Congressional staff will add it to the tally of pros and cons shown to the representative in the House or Senate. A personal, handwritten letter will receive even more attention. Form letters are not taken nearly as seriously.

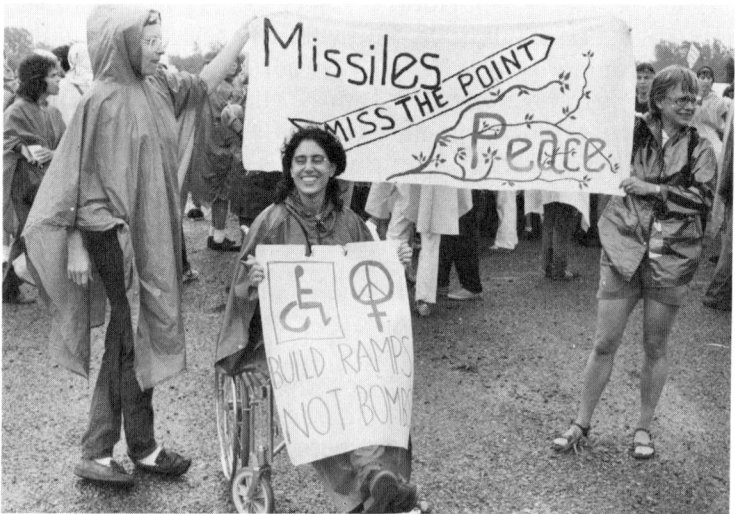

Three thousand women gather in the rain at Sampson State Park to march for peace, August 1, 1983. Photo by Nancy Clover © 1983.

Here are some tips about how to write an effective letter to a member of Congress:

1. Start with a positive comment, perhaps commending your representative's willingness to receive citizen opinion.

2. Show you know something about your representative's

stand on military issues by mentioning a recent speech, vote, or newspaper comment by him or her. If you don't know how he or she stands on the issue, ask.

3. Relate a personal story about the way nuclear war concerns or frightens your family, or how you and your family have to tighten your belts while high Pentagon spending continues to fuel inflation and increase the tax burden. Don't hesitate to take a moral or religious stand, or to relate a conversation, a nightmare, a personal insight, or your reaction to a TV program or film.

4. Focus in on specific issues—a proposed new weapon system, the new Pentagon budget, a treaty or other bill. State your own position clearly, and ask your representative to do likewise. Don't feel you have to be an expert. There is nothing wrong with saying, "I'm no military expert, but this new . . . missile just doesn't make any sense!"

5. Suggest to your representative where he or she can turn for accurate, expert information, independent of the Pentagon and military contractors.

6. Ask your representative if he or she would be willing to meet with people in your community to discuss the issue of nuclear war.

7. Tell your representative that you are deeply concerned about nuclear war and hope for a personal reply rather than a form letter.

8. Save all the rest of your ideas for the next letter—don't try to cover more than one issue at one time!

9. Feel free to enclose an informative newspaper clipping . . . or other substantive information. Congressional offices are very busy, so don't assume the staff already has the information.

10. Put a legible return address and phone number on your letter. Envelopes get thrown away. Sign your letter. . . .[4]

There may not always be enough time or information to do all of these things in a single letter. However, they provide a good general guideline. Remember, try to keep your letter brief (usually less than one page) and focused on one issue that will soon be coming before the Congress or Senate.

Here is the suggested format that Bread for the World uses.[5]

President . . . .
The White House
Washington, DC 20501

Representative . . . .
House Office Building
Washington, DC 20515

Senator . . . .
Senate Office Building
Washington, DC 20510

Dear Senator . . . :   Dear Representative . . . :   Dear President . . . :

Begin with a commendation on a past vote or speech.

Identify the legislation clearly. Give the bill number (and title and author if known) and the stage of the bill in the legislative process. Do not assume the legislator will know the bill you are writing about.

State your reason for writing. Personal experience is the best supporting evidence. Explain what effect the bill will have on you, your community, or your state. If available, offer documented evidence or statistics in support of your views.

Raise questions; they are more likely to encourage a response. The more challenging your letter, the better the chance of reaching someone of influence, thus avoiding a routine response or form letter.

Thank you for your consideration of my views.

Sincerely,

A Concerned Citizen

If you want to register your opinion quickly to your Senator or Representative about an imminent vote, phone (202) 224-3121. To call the White House with an opinion, you can phone (202) 456-7639. A telegram can also be a good attention-getter, especially immediately before a key vote. They are usually counted "for" and "against," so make them brief, concise, and include the bill number.

A personal visit to your congressperson is the most effective means of contact. A visit to the local or Washington office can easily be arranged. Before visiting her congressperson, one creative woman sent the representative a pecan pie with one thin slice removed from the pan. She included a note that said, "There's important legislation coming up to focus attention on the fact that the poor don't get their fair share of the pie. . . . "[6] Determine the length of the visit (usually 10 to 30 minutes) prior to the appointment and plan how to utilize that time in the most effective way. It is best to meet with a member of Congress at the beginning of each new session and at least once again during the year, taking advantage of periodic congressional recesses.

Elected representatives usually keep an eye on their local and national newspapers, television, and radio to see how the public feels about an issue on which they will soon vote. The media also has an effect on the views of citizens who then may make their opinions known to the representatives. It is important to provide factual information to the public that may be otherwise omitted. Write letters to the editor. Encourage the newspapers, TV, and radio to keep people informed. You may even suggest specific events that should be covered or films that should be shown. Public TV and radio are particularly open to suggestions regarding public service programming.

Action for Communities

Coordinated action by the religious community, with its enormous resources, can play a critical role in reshaping US policies and actions toward reversal of the arms race and seeking alternative ways to defend the nation. Christian groups meeting together—worshiping, studying, praying, and taking action—can help to make the world more peaceful.

When Christians work together for a common good,

great things can happen. The local church is in a unique situation to make a difference for the following reasons:

1. The congregation includes a wider cross-section of American public opinion than most organizations have.
2. A supportive fellowship is present in congregations in which individuals can test out new opinions and attitudes in an accepting atmosphere. The local church provides an environment where change is possible.
3. The authoritative basis for theological thinking for Christian disciples is the Bible. The Bible gives a rationale and a call for peacemaking.
4. With its denominational ties, the congregation is connected to a wide network of other church groups. One local church can influence a number of other churchs through this network.
5. The congregation can play a role as a moral leader within its community when it elects to do so. Lay and clergy associations have shown ability to influence community decision-making.
6. Lay people in congregations are already involved in the world's corporate structures, in government positions, in the military, and in voting booths—vital locations to bring about changes on behalf of peace.[7]

Individuals can increase their effectiveness by working with others, supporting one another, and challenging each other's approaches to issues. They can give strong moral and spiritual support to one another's various forms of peace work. It is also important and helpful for congregations and small groups to become affiliated with one or more of the national organizations that are working on issues of peace and justice.

Often, congregations do not want to become involved in issues of peace and justice. One church member put it this way,

Many people come to church "to feel good," and they don't want to be bothered with tough world issues . . . However, Jesus didn't get killed because he made people smile a lot.

Much as I enjoy coffee hour, the cross—and not the coffee pot—still dominates the sanctuary.[8]

When working in groups, there is power in numbers but there is also that much feared word—"bureaucracy"! It is far too easy to get bogged down in organizational details or side issues. It is not necessary to spend several meetings drawing up a "statement of principles" or trying to agree on all the issues. Then there are the groups that try to do everything without enough deliberation; soon people realize that they are overcommitted and they drop out altogether. Some groups have one or two leaders who try to do everything themselves without getting others involved. Others try to "organize their communities" without realizing that the community is already organized into groups such as schools, labor unions, religious bodies, and Chambers of Commerce. Much more can be done by "plugging in" to these existing groups, helping them to spend some time discussing issues of war and peace. This can be done in the form of a film, speech, or display.

Peacemaking does not consist of projects, meetings, demonstrations, and petitions alone. It must include the building of community and be based on prayer. Community —the intimate, loving, face-to-face encounter with our sisters and brothers—provides a space for the Spirit to work in us and empowers us to work for peace. Without community and prayer, we are isolated individuals shouting into the wind. Uniting together with each other and with God, we have the power to change the world.

Prayer

The alternative to the nuclear arms race and the action suggestions mentioned in this book should be considered prayerfully. Prayer is in itself a very important step in working for peace in the nuclear era.

George Kennan told students at Princeton Theological Seminary that in the long run Christians have no choice but to throw themselves on the mercy of God. He was not, however, crying out his despair. On the contrary, his statement grew out of a recognition, based on his analysis of the present situation, that humanity might yet be saved if, through the mercy of God, humanity is protected from fatal political folly, military stupidity, and nuclear accidents. From such dangers as these, we have "nowhere to turn but to Heaven."[9]

Jesus Christ specifically commanded his disciples to pray for their enemies. 1 Timothy 2:1-2 makes it clear that the first duty of every gathered congregation is to pray for their national leaders so that they "may lead a quiet and peaceable life." Think of the power of the whole church family uniting in fervent, concentrated prayer for rulers, for enemies, and for peace, freedom, and justice in the world!

The Catholic Bishops' letter encourages Christians to pray, beseeching the risen Christ to fill the world with his peace. They particularly advocate contemplative prayer because it advances harmony and peace in the world:

> For this prayer rises, by divine grace, where there is total disarmament of the heart and unfolds in an experience of love which is the moving force of peace. Contemplation fosters a vision of the human family as united and interdependent in the mystery of God's love for all people . . . We implore . . . Christians and everyone of good will to join us in this continuing prayer for peace, as we beseech God for peace within ourselves, in our families and community, in our nation, and in the world.[10]

Prayer is not passive; it is an active response to the present nuclear danger. At a time when there is growing concern and many persons are feeling helpless, hopeless, and confused about what to do, Christians must be moved to pray and moved by that prayer. The nuclear threat should drive Christians to a new depth and intensity of prayer. Through prayer, we place ourselves in God's hands. As we begin to understand that our security is in God only, we become less dependent upon the false securities that enslave us and lead to war. Prayer frees us from our spiritual bondage to property, money, power, and ideas, and from the causes which have made us willing to destroy everything in a desperate and futile effort to protect them.

Jim Wallis, editor of *Sojourners Magazine,* has written:

> Only those who have truly found their security in God can resist the violent tugs and pulls of the false securities offered by the nuclear powers. By re-establishing our security in God, prayer can become an effective weapon in combatting those powers.[11]

Here are some suggestions about prayer and peacemaking:

1. Incorporate worship in study groups, homes, and other settings; include opportunities for listening to God to discern the signs and bonds of peace, and to celebrate them.

2. Plan for structured times of prayer and reflection in worship and group meetings to focus attention on persons and situations across the globe. Seek out and meditate upon God's will for people near and far who are victimized by injustice, war, and the threat of violence.

3. Ask groups and individuals to name those they would call their enemies. Suggest they pray for guidance in building bonds of peace. . . .

4. Ask persons to work individually or in groups to write a "Peace Pledge" and use these pledges in worship and prayer times. . . .

5. Select hymns and special songs for worship and prayer sessions that celebrate the themes of righteousness and harmony as central to Christian discipleship. . . .

6. Select a nation that is currently caught in the grip of war's destructiveness. Study the nation's history, the story of its people, and the causes of the current strife. Take time to pray for the people of that land and for their deliverance from violence and oppression. . . .

7. Pray for national and world leaders, for unknown persons working for peace with justice, for soldiers and children who yearn for the signs of peace and seek to work together to build bonds of peace.

8. Read Amos 5:24 and Luke 18-19. Pray that God might

speak to us today, instructing and guiding us so that we might know the way of peace with justice as faithful disciples of Jesus Christ.[12]

When actions against the arms race are not based on the act of prayer, they can become fearful, fanatical, bitter, and more an expression of survival instincts than of faith in God as the God of the living. When prayer remains the act from which all actions flow, Christians can be joyful even when times are depressing, peaceful even when the threat of war is all around, and hopeful even when constantly tempted to despair. The world no longer has power over them.

> Then justice will dwell in the
>   wilderness, and
>   righteousness abide in the
>   fruitful field.
> And the effect of
>   righteousness will be peace,
>   and the result of
>   righteousness quietness and
>   trust forever.
> My people will abide in
>   peaceful habitation, in
>   secure dwellings, and in
>   quiet resting places.
>   — Isaiah 32:16-18

Postscript

Calligraphy by Lawrence Romorini

A Visit to A Loving and Just Society

What would an ideal future look like? When people have a better idea of what they want the world to be like, then they will have a goal toward which to work.

For many people, it is hard to imagine a wonderful future because it seems so unrealistic to them. However, it is through dreaming and following their dreams that many great inventors and humanitarians realized great goals.

Martin Luther King, Jr. said, "I have a dream . . . " Look how far it brought the world! Children often come up with creative ideas because they are not as inhibited by what is supposedly too unusual to work. Dare to let your mind expand. Let the Holy Spirit work through your creative energies.

The following essay is an example of what a loving and just society might look like. Before reading it, think a bit about how you would like the world to be. Think about future schools, food, homes, transportation, relationships, cities, and families. Don't focus on what you fear they will be like, but imagine what they would look like if your dreams came true.

I had finished building my time machine a couple of weeks ago. I had been building it in my grandparents' old garage. The idea to make it came while I was day-dreaming in physics class. It was a lot of fun to create, using parts that came mainly from my brother's junk yard. It was a weird looking contraption. Pieces of pipe and bumpers stuck out everywhere. I added a horn and useless steering wheel just for the fun of it. It's amazing that the thing actually did work. At one point when I was traveling in it, I felt as though the bolts would shake out and the whole thing would fall apart. But this is not what I wanted to tell you about.

I do want to tell you about the wonderful society I saw when visiting the future. I still get goose bumps just thinking about it. Let me start at the beginning . . .

Sitting in the time machine, I adjusted the "possible futures" knob. You see, there are an infinite number of possible futures. The future we will have depends on what we do in the present. This machine can take me to various possible futures, and then I can ask the people in that time period what had to happen in order to make their society become the way it is.

I set the knob on the possible future marked "Loving and Just Society." At first nothing happened. I figured something must have been miscalculated. But after a minute, everything started shaking, the headlights blinked on and off. Suddenly I was surrounded by total darkness. There was a huge gravitational pull and then I fainted . . .

Upon awakening, I was still in the time machine. It was located on the top of a large building. Fortunately there was also a large tree next to the building which I could reach from the roof. I swung onto one of the branches and climbed down. There was little time to explore because in six hours the machine had been preset to return to my grandparents' garage in my own time period, with or without me.

Walking around this attractive modern building, I soon came to the front entrance. The sign above the door said, "Langley Junior High School." Slowly and quietly I walked down a hallway and listened outside of one of the classroom doors. Straining my ears, I could hear the teacher say, "Aristotle wanted to locate justice within the character of a person. He stressed that people are 'just' only if they perform just acts by choice and voluntarily. Aristotle argued that learning to act justly is tied to friendship. Friendship is more central in the moral life than justice; it is what holds states together. Our friends help us learn what it means to be just. Justice is part of friendship. Justice strives for equality. Friendship goes a step farther—to love."

The children then rearranged their chairs to form small groups. Older youth, probably high school seniors, helped to lead each small group discussion on what the teacher had been saying. Each group was also supposed to pick a project to do in order to demonstrate justice and friendship in their own homes. All of the groups were talking at once. It was impossible to hear anything so I went on down the hall.

After leaving the school I decided to take a walk around the neighborhood. I was surprised that there weren't many cars. From the bus and subway signs, it appeared that mass transportation had become very popular. I soon came to a well-kept park with lots of preschoolers playing on swings and playground equipment. A newspaper was laying on a vacant bench. Quickly I went over to take a look. The headlines were amazing. There was no mention of murder, robbery, or other crimes which I had often found in papers back home. There was no mention of wars, or chemical waste problems or other devestations. Instead, the news was about world conferences that were taking place to assure continued peace, about new ideas for greater food production, about improved trade laws being implemented, about medical ideas being tested to help prevent birth defects and catastrophic illnesses. The paper also included the "Daily Good Samaritan Story." Apparently, each day the paper included a story about some self-sacrificial act that someone had done to help others.

I decided to talk with a man who was watching the children play. He seemed friendly enough. I asked him about the billboard sign I had seen that had "Shalom" written on it.

"You must not be from around here," he responded with a

smile. "Shalom is a Hebrew word used in the Old Testament. It means "peace with justice." We define it as creating an economy that is not based upon armaments; envisioning a world in which every man and woman has access to meaningful and creative work, and helping to bring about a world in which no one is disinherited and powerless. To work toward shalom is to work for economic justice, equality for ethnic minorities and women, and the elimination of world hunger — as well as continued disarmament and world peace. The billboards with : 'Shalom' help remind us of the kind of world for which we want."

"But . . . but I thought this already *was* a loving and just society," I cried. "Why do you need to work toward a world of shalom? Don't you already have it?

"You really aren't from around here," he said, eyeing me questioningly. "Of course we don't have a perfect world of shalom. That will never happen until after we're dead or until The Kingdom of God comes — if at all. Humans fall short of God's love, and so we are naturally going to make mistakes. Things are a lot better than they used to be, though, and more and more people are letting God work through them to make this world a better place."

He then offered to take me on a tour to show me a little about his society. Curious, I inquired who would look after the children in the park. He explained that a substitute from the community would be available to come care for them. He pressed a few buttons on the side of his wrist watch and talked into the face of it. When I heard a voice respond through the watch, I realized that it must be some kind of telephone. While we waited for his replacement, I asked him to tell me more about the community to which he had referred.

"This society consists of many, many smaller communities, or household living groups. The communities vary in size, depending upon the needs and desires of its participants. I prefer my medium-sized community that's small enough so that you can know everyone yet large enough for plenty of new and exciting things to happen. We continually try to make our communities more and more inclusive of people of various races, ages, and backgrounds. We have so much to learn from each other. One of the hardest tasks for us when these communities first got going was to get people to really listen to and try to understand others who came from different perspectives. There's still much work to be done in this area. Unfortunately, some communities are less friendly to new people than they should be.

"In our communities, we try to live simple life-styles. We

realize that we live in a world of limits and scarce goods. In a world where everyone cannot be wealthy, we must try to close the huge gap between rich and poor. The rich must live more simply so that the poor may simply live.[2] We've found that we are actually happier without a lot of unnecessary material possessions that advertising used to tell us that we needed. There is a lot of sharing and trading that goes on between communities, but due to time and energy things are mostly done within one's own group.

"Within our communiities, we share just about everything, including child care responsibilities. We take turns watching the pre-school children during school hours so that parents can work during the day and then be with all of their children after school. Sandy agreed to substitute for me today when I told her I wanted to give you a tour. We share household equipment such as ladders, washing machines, paint brushes, and lawn mowers as well. Who needs to own things that they only use every now and then? All of us feel free to borrow anything from anyone as long as they aren't using it at that time and as long as we don't damage it.

"Many jobs are shared. We take turns doing the laundry, gardening, and washing the dishes. That reminds me—we often have meals together as a community, though most of our meals are with our smaller families. Those who have no real family are usually "adopted" in an informal way by a family that has grown particularly fond of them. No one, then, is without a support system and no one goes hungry.

"On the other hand, no one is allowed to be lazy or encouraged to take things without contributing. One rule that all of the communities have is that everyone who has the ability to work, can and will have a job. We've found that unless someone is very ill, there's always something they can do to help. We have workshops for the retarded and the handicapped that teach them skills that they can perform. They contribute to the community and are challenged to become their best selves."

These communities sounded wonderful. While we were discussing them, Sandy arrived to watch the children. Soon Jerry and I were on our way to a beautiful church where he knew they were having a Bible study. "What denomination is this?" I asked as we entered.

"Denomination . . . denomination? Oh yes, you mean like Catholic, Presbyterian, Methodist—that sort of thing? We don't have denominations as such any more. This is a "Christian" church. Of course, there are disagreements about things like how the eucharist should be observed, how the church should be governed, what type of architecture is most appropriate, and what kind of liturgy should be used. Each local church still has its own style of worship. However, we are slowly working it out. People feel strongly enough that we are all one body of Christ that they are willing to work hard toward ecumenism."

Jerry took me through the sanctuary of the church. I saw that it was set up for a communion service. I asked if they had the eucharist often.

"Yes. It is one of the most important aspects of worship. When we participate in the eucharist, we are declaring our unity as a holy people across all nations and across past, present, and future."[3]

"The eucharist changes the way we live. We take what people like David Hallenbach have said seriously. It goes something like this:

When Christians partake of the eucharist, they are graced wth a concrete manifestation of the shape of God's covenent with all humanity. This covenant is realized in the sharing of food. There is an intrinsic affinity between the Christian sacramental imagination and the assertion that all humans have a right to food. Taking the eucharist does not inform us of specific political or structural actions that we should take to assure everyone's right to food. However, it helps us to affirm this right and to see that there is a need for us to look at political and structural changes.

Yep, Hollenbach sure knew what he was talking about when he wrote about that."[4]

"Is there still a problem with world hunger?" I asked. "Is everyone in the world well-fed?"

Here in the United States we've pretty much eliminated the problem of hunger and malnutrition, but there's still much more to do in the world. We're making a lot of progress."

"What did you do to get rid of hunger here and what is being done about the world?"

"The key to wiping out hunger in our country was through forming more and more communities until everyone had a support system and a place to contribute. The hardest part was convincing the wealthy that it was in the best interests of all to join a community which included sharing their personal possessions. However, many of them were Christians who slowly came to see the need to share in a community.

"To help alleviate the problem of hunger in other countries, we are moving toward an international economic order. We have found that even strong nations benefit when they give weak nations the opportunity to become stronger and to build a more healthy world economy. This international economic order includes the way we deal with trade terms, debt burdens, armaments that take food from the mouths of the poor, international lending agencies, aid programs, and so forth. Revamping the structure of the world economic order is just as important as providing relief, localized economic aid, or some form of charity."[5]

I asked Jerry what he thought about churches that are engaged in political activities. I had always heard that there should be separation of church and state.

"Christians should not avoid involvement in politics," Jerry responded, "Christians should recognize, however, that politics inherently involves compromise and accommodation. To withdraw from the political in order "to remain pure" is an irresponsible act of despair, and it is self-deceptive because it creates the condition by which the political realm may claim unwarranted significance. However, in Christian enthusiasm for political involvement offered by our secular polity, the church must not forget its more profound political task. Christians need to challenge the moral presuppositions of our polity and society. There can be no just polity without people being just. Genuine justice depends on more profound moral convictions than our secular polity can politically acknowledge."[6]

We left the church and walked toward the downtown area. I noticed how beautiful the city was. The architects had been careful to include plenty of plants and pictures within and around the buildings. Buildings were made inexpensively, yet sturdily and with imagination. We passed some young people who were painting a lovely mural on a side wall as part of their afterschool class project. I remembered how nice the park was and how clean everything seemed. The buildings were made to serve large populations efficiently, but they were also made to be pleasing to the senses. When I asked Jerry about this, he replied:

"When people create an ugly environment, they destroy part of themselves. Our cities shape us. Aesthetic delight in the world is a gift from God, a gift which we should enjoy. Instead of making our cities 'machines for living,' we plan and build them to the delight of our senses. When we are in an attractive environment, our spirits are lifted and we find ourselves being kinder to one another."[7]

As we wandered through a peace museum, my stomach began to rumble. I was quite embarrassed. Jerry smiled at me, his eyes laughing. "Come on," he gave me a gentle tug toward the exit door. "I bet you haven't eaten since breakfast."

We walked to a nearby co-op grocery and picked up some yogurt, mixed nuts, and apple juice. Jerry told me that there were co-ops all over. They help to keep prices down and folks that belonged to them usually became good friends.

While in the co-op, I saw a poster of a black teenager helping an older white woman to get up. The woman looked as though she had just slipped on the icy street. Under the picture were these words: "Bonhoeffer said that when the neighbor is actually loved for hi/er own sake and when there is genuine love, then God is being known and loved—not as another 'object,' but in the quality of the relationship."[8] I asked Jerry what the strange word in the poster, "hi/er," meant. He explained that it was a contraction for "his or her." Apparently, there were several new words that helped to make the English language more inclusive. Jerry said it was hard for people to get used to the new words at first but that it now seemed quite natural to use such contractions.

Suddenly, I heard yelling coming from the back of the co-op. One man was yelling at another, his face flaming in anger. I couldn't understand what he said, but it was something about the other man sleeping with his wife. The next thing I knew, they were fighting. One man, dodging the other's blow, backed into the vegetable cart. Tomatoes, cucumbers, carrots, and other vegetables were rolling everywhere. Next, barrels of flour and sugar came crashing down off the shelves. Almost instantly, the co-op members near the two men intervened. Three people escorted one man out the front door and three took the other man out the back. The woman at the cash register and Jerry looked quite embarrassed. "This is quite, quite unusual," he said.

"They broke the law because they damaged public property. When anyone breaks a law, they are taken to meet with counselors. The counselors try to determine what motivated the person to break the law and what needs to be done. In this case, the counselors will try and help the men talk out their problems. Then, as a punishment, they will be given some extra duties to do. In this case, they will probably be required to clean up the mess they made in the co-op and to raise enough money to replace the damaged goods."

"What if someone commits murder?" I asked.

"That kind of crime almost never happens around here because we try to catch things before they get too bad. For example, we teach people how to talk out their problems and we have classes on conflict resolution. Everyone has the support and necessities of life so there is no need to steal. Most people are satisfied with what they have. Each community encourages its members to keep the laws, by trying to stop people early when they first start going astray. However, as you can tell, sometimes people's emotions get the best of them and they do things that they shouldn't. If they are not willing to cooperate and they are dangerous to others, then we do have to put them in rehabilitation centers temporarily."

"What about violence on a larger scale?" I wondered aloud. "Are there any wars or revolts in this society?"

"This society is quite peaceful now. We have stopped the nuclear arms race and slowly the world is coming to peaceful agreements, bargaining away the nuclear weapons that we have all built. We have international exchange programs with those who have been our enemies or who are potential enemies. We're trying to understand each other better. We're helping other countries to start national peace academies like the one we've had for years. Our peace academy searches for peace in national policy, does research on conflict resolution, educates the public on issues of war and peace, and is a tangible symbol of the United States' commitment to building world peace.

"Peace is not something to be achieved by our power alone. Rather, peace is a gift of God that comes only by our being a community formed around a crucified savior — a savior who teaches us how to be peaceful in a world in rebellion against its true Lord. God's peaceful kingdom, we are learning, comes not by positing a common human morality, but by our faithfulness as a peaceful community that does not fear differences. We have learned to be patient in the face of injustice rather than to use violence.[9] Violence only breeds more violence."

I glanced at my watch and was surprised to see that almost six hours had passed. I had to get back to the time machine before it went back to my own time. Jerry walked me quickly back toward the junior high school.

I could see the school up ahead. We neared the tree, and I prepared to climb up it to get into the machine that sat on the roof. Fortunately, it was just out of sight from the ground so no one had noticed it. When I thanked Jerry for all that he had taught me, he said I was welcome to stay and join his community.

For a moment, I considered staying. I thought of what a wonderful society this was. People were so nice to each other; they really cared. So many problems had been worked out and they were still working to make the world even better. I could really be happy here.

Then I thought of people in my own time. What would happen to them if I didn't go back and tell them about how wonderful the future could be if they worked toward a loving and just society? What if my people continued in the direction that they were heading and there was a huge nuclear war? I realized that if I shared with the people in my time the ways in which we can work together with each other and with God to build a wonderful society . . .

Here I am back at home. I'm typing this so that people can read it and hopefully decide to do something towards building a better world. There are so many different possible futures. Perhaps we can join together and help make peace and justice a reality . . .

Does this story spur any new ideas for your future? Think some more about how you would want the future to be. Then initiate a study group, discuss the example, and share your own visions with each other. Remember not to criticize one another's ideas. In the past, some of the craziest sounding ideas turned out to lead to important discoveries. Help each other to clarify. Listen and share. Don't forget—have fun with it; the author imagines that the future will be filled with laughter and joy.

Appendix

Resource Agencies and Organizations

American Friends Service Committee (AFSC), 1501 Cherry Street, Philadelphia, PA 19102

Amnesty International, 304 West 58 St., New York, NY 10019

Arms Control Association, 11 Dupont Circle, NW, Washington, DC 20036

Bread for the World, 802 Rhode Island Ave., NE, Washington, DC 20018

CARECEN (Central American Refugee Center), 3112 Mt. Pleasant St., NW, Washington, DC 20010

Center for Defense Information, 122 Maryland Avenue, NE, Washington, DC 20002

Center on Law and Pacifism, P.O. Box 1584, Colorado Springs, CO 80901

Central Committee for Conscientious Objectors, 2208 South St., Philadelphia, PA 19146

Children's Defense Fund, 122 C St., NW, Washington, DC 20001

Clergy and Laity Concerned, 198 Broadway, New York, NY 10038

Council on Economic Priorities, 84 Fifth Ave., New York, NY 10011

Disarmament Program, American Friends Service Comm., 1501 Cherry St., Philadelphia, PA 19102

Fellowship of Reconciliation (FOR), Box 271, Nyack, N\ 10960

Institute for Global Education, 25 Sheldon Blvd., Ste. 314, Grand Rapids, MI 49503

Interfaith Center to Reverse the Arms Race, 132 N. Euclid Ave., Pasadena, CA 91101

Jobs with Peace, 77 Summer St., Suite 1111, Boston, MA 02110

Leadership Conference of Women Religious, 8808 Cameron St., Silver Spring, MD 20910

Mennonite Central Committee, Peace Section, 21 S. 12th Street, Akron, PA 17501

Mobilization for Survival, 853 Broadway, Rm. 2109, New York, NY 10003

National Council of Churches, 110 Maryland Ave., NE, Washington DC 20002

National Interreligious Service Board for Conscientious Objectors, 550 Washington Bldg., Washington, DC 20005

National Peace Academy Campaign, 110 Maryland Ave., NE, Washington, DC 20002

New Call to Peacemaking, Box 1245, Elkhart, IN 46515

Partners for Global Justice, The Interaction Center, 4920 Piney Brance Rd., NW, Washington, DC 20011

Pax Christi-USA, 8000 N. Mango Ave., Chicago, IL 60634

Peacemakers, Box 627, Garberville, CA 95440

The Peace Museum, 364 W. Erie St., Chicago, IL 60610

Physicians for Social Responsibility, 639 Massachusetts Ave., Cambridge, MA 02139

Presbyterian Church, USA, The Presbyterian Distribution Service, 905 Interchurch Center, 475 Riverside Dr., New York, NY 10015

SANE: A Citizens' Organization for a Sane World, 514 C Street, NW, Washington, DC 20002

Sojourners, P.O. Box 29272, NW, Washington, DC 20017

War Resisters League, 339 Lafayett St., New York, NY 10012

Washington Peace Center, 2111 Florida Ave., NW, Washington, DC 20008

Women's International League for Peace and Freedom, 1213 Race Street, Philadelphia, PA 19107

World Disarmament Campaign Center for Disarmament, Liaison Office, United Nations, New York, NY 10017

World Ministries Commission, Church of the Brethren General Board, 1451 Dundee Ave., Elgin, IL 60120

World Peace Tax Fund, 2121 Decatur Place, NW, Washington, DC 20008

World Peacemakers, 2025 Massachusetts Ave., NW, Washington, DC 20036

World Without War Council, 421 S. Wabash, Chicago, IL 60605

Notes

Chapter 1: Blessed are the Peacemakers

1. Jim Wallis, "A Dream. (Sometime in the future . . .)," *Sojourners* (August, 1980).
2. Roger Shinn, "Faith, Science, Ideology and the Nuclear Decision," in *Riverside Disarmament Reader: A Model Course for Disarmament Studies,* George Hunsinger, editor (New York: Riverside Church Disarmament Program, 1980).
3. Alan Geyer, *The Maze of Peace* (New York: Friendship Press, 1969), p. 17.

Chapter 2: Pacifism

1. Foster Bittinger, "The Pacifist and his Power for Good," reprinted from *Brethren Bible Study Monthly,* Feb. 1957, p. 1.
2. New Call to Peacemaking. "Statement of the Findings Committee" (Green Lake, WI, Oct., 1978), p. 1.
3. Roland Bainton, *Christian Attitudes Toward War and Peace* (Nashville: Abingdon Press, 1960), p. 153.
4. Bainton, p. 153.
5. Umphrey Lee, *The Historical Church and Modern Pacifism* (Nashville: Abingdon-Cokesbury Press, 1943), p. 156.
6. Lee, p. 159.
7. Dan West, *A Four-Session Unit of Peace Studies* (Elgin, IL: A Brethren Service Social Education Publication, 1958), p. 5.
8. *Annual Conference and General Brotherhood Board Statements: 1947-1961* (Elgin, IL, 1962). The most recent statement on war was adopted in 1970.
9. *Problems of War and Peace* (Hamilton, New York: Colgate University Press, 1980), pp. 248, 249.
10. David Hollenbach, *Nuclear Ethics: A Christian Moral Argument* (New York: Paulist Press, 1983), p. 23.
11. Hollenbach, p. 26.
12. Larry Rasmussen, "The Nuclear Dilemma," Wesley Theological Seminary, 1984, pp. 14, 15.
13. Dale Aukerman, Shalom Tract No. 4, Available from Brethren Peace Fellowship.
14. *The Facts . . . About the Alternative Services Program of the Brethren Service Commission.* (ELgin, IL: General Brotherhood Board, n.d.)
15. "If You Work for Peace, Stop Paying for War," Available from National War Tax Resistance Coordinating Committee (NWTRCC), P.O. Box 2236, East Patchogue, NY 11772.

16. "Your Telephone Tax Pays for War!" Available from NWTRCC.
17. "1983 Annual Conference Statement on War Tax Consultation," Available from Church of the Brethren General Offices, Elgin, IL.
18. "Faith & Taxes," Available from National Campaign for a US Peace Tax Fund, 2121 Decatur Place, NW, Washington, DC 20008.
19. "Faith & Taxes."
20. Donald F. Durnbaugh, ed., *Meet The Brethren* (Elgin, IL: Brethren Press for The Brethren Encyclopedia, Inc., 1984), p. 80.
21. "CCCO Annual Report 1982," Available from CCCO.
22. New Call to Peacemaking, p. 1.

Chapter 3: The Crusade Against Communism

1. Anthony Lewis, "Nukes: An issue of politics, not religion," *Detroit Free Press,* March 10, 1983.
2. Roland Bainton, pp. 45, 46.
3. Justo Gonzalez, *The Story of Christianity,* Volume 1 (San Francisco: Harper & Row, 1984), pp. 292, 293.
4. Gonzalez, p. 296.
5. Daniel Maguire, *The Moral Choice* (Garden City, NY: Doubleday and Co., 1978), p. 70.
6. Bainton, p. 56.
7. Bainton, p. 56.
8. Gonzalez, pp. 296–300.
9. "Evangelical Association Refuses Stand on Peace," *Michigan Christian Advocate,* March 24, 1983, p. 7.
10. Robert Webber, "The Moral Majority: Right or Wrong?" (speech presented at Albion College Convocation, Albion, MI, Feb. 17, 1983).
11. Webber.
12. George Church, "How Reagan Decides," *Time Magazine,* December 13, 1982, p. 17.
13. Church, p. 17.
14. "Reagan: Preach against Freeze," *USA TODAY,* March 9, 1983.
15. Lewis, p. 6A.
16. Helen Caldicott, Plenary Speech at The Second Biennial Conference on the Fate of the Earth, Sept. 22, 1984.
17. Lewis.
18. Bishop Armstrong, "In a Dark Time . . . " in *Orientation–82* (Nashville: Board of Higher Education and Ministry, United Methodist Church, 1982), p. 6.
19. Charles Morrison, *The Christian and the War* (Chicago: Willett, Clark and Co., 1942), p. 142.
20. Jacques Ellul, *Violence: Reflections from a Christian Perspective* (New York: The Seabury Press, 1969), p. 137.
21. Ellul, pp. 137, 138.

Chapter 4: The Just War Theory

1. Ruth Benedict, *The 1983 War Resisters League Calendar.*

2. John Yoder, *When War is Unjust* (Minneapolis: Augsburg Publishing House, 1984), p. 9.
3. Paul Ramsey, *War and the Christian Conscience: How Shall Modern War Be Conducted Justly?* (Durham, NC: Duke University Press, 1961), xxiii.
4. Gonzalez, p. 214.
5. Rasmussen, p. 16.
6. David Hollenbach, *Nuclear Ethics: A Christian Moral Argument* (New York: Paulist Press, 1983), pp. 34, 38.
7. Donald Strobe, "Live Peaceably, If Possible," *Michigan Christian Advocate*, Oct. 21, 1982, p. 3.
8. Hollenbach, pp. 16–23.
9. Hollenbach, pp. 25–26.
10. Rasmussen, p. 18.
11. John Bennett, *When Christians Make Political Decisions* (New York: Association Press, 1964), pp. 76, 77.
12. Strobe, p. 3.
13. Ramsey, pp. 190, 191.
14. Ramsey, p. xx.
15. Ramsey, p. viii.
16. Strobe, p. 3.
17. Strobe, p. 3.
18. Jacques Ellul, *Violence*, p. 7.
19. Ellul, pp. 6, 7.
20. Ellul, pp. 106, 114.
21. As quoted in Ellul, p. 111.
22. Ellul, p. 111.
23. Thomas Aquinas, *Summa Theologia II–II*, p. 40, cited by J. Bryan Hehir in "The Just-War Ethic and Catholic Theology: Dynamics of Change and Continuity," *War or Peace? The Search for Answers*, Thomas A. Shannon, editor (Maryknoll, NY: Orbis Books, 1980), p. 18.
24. Yoder, p. 41.

Chapter 5: The Nuclear War Era

1. Anne Meyer, *Nuclear War and Christian Faithfulness* (Senior paper, Goshen College, Goshen, Indiana, 1980), p. 1. Available from World Peacemakers.
2. Ramsey, p. vii.
3. Meyer, p. 1.
4. John Bennett, *Nuclear Weapons and the Conflict of Conscience* (New York: Charles Scribner's Sons, 1962), p. 41.
5. Richard McSorley, "It's a Sin to Build a Nuclear Weapon," in *Riverside Disarmament Reader*.
6. Ground Zero, *Nuclear War: What's In It For You?* (New York: Pocket Books, 1982), p. 76.
7. "Call to Halt the Nuclear Arms Race: Proposal for a Mutual US—Soviet Nuclear-Weapon Freeze," Available from Clergy and Laity Concerned.

8. James Muller, *The 1983 War Resisters League Calendar and Appointment Book,* Maris Cakers, editor (New York: War Resisters League, 1982).

9. Nuclear Weapons Freeze Campaign, "US Defense Experts on Pershing II," in Euromissile Packet.

10. McSorley.

11. *The 1983 War Resisters League Calendar,* November.

12. Stott.

13. Strobe, p. 3.

14. Strobe, p. 3.

15. The Independent Commission on Disarmament and Security Issues, *Common Security: A Blueprint for Survival* (New York: Simon and Schuster, 1982), pp. 16–18.

16. Gordon Zahn, *An Alternative to War* (New York: The Council on Religion and International Affairs, 1963), pp. 14, 15.

17. Jim Wallis, *The Call to Conversion: Recovering the Gospel for These Times* (San Francisco: Harper & Row, 1982), p. 74.

18. Wallis, *Call to Conversion,* p. 75.

19. David Hainer, "A Christmas Eve Dream," *The Michigan Christian Advocate,* December 24, 1984, p. 5.

20. World Peacemakers, *Building Christian Community: Pursuing Peace with Justice,* 1983, p. 29.

21. Meyer, p. 4.

Chapter 6: Three Religious Perspectives on Nuclear War

1. Michael Walzer, *Just and Unjust Wars: A Moral Argument with Historical Illustrations* (New York: Basic Books, Inc., 1977), p. 279.

2. "Nuclear Freeze: A Necessary First Step,;; *The Defense Monitor* (Washington, DC: Center for Defense Information, 1982).

3. John Bennett, *Moral Tensions in International Affairs* (New York: The Council on Religion and International Affairs, 1964), p. 23.

4. "Resolution on the World Arms Race, 1978," Available from Peace Section (US), Mennonite Central Committee.

5. Wallis, *The Call to Conversion* p. 88.

6. Ramsey, pp. 138, 193, 277, 278.

7. Ramsey, pp. 275, 276.

8. Ramsey, p. 227.

9. Ramsey, p. 60.

10. Paul Ramsey, *The Limits of Nuclear War: Thinking about the Do-able and the Un-do-able* (New York: The Council on Religion and International Affairs, 1963), p. 11.

11. Ramsey, *Limits of Nuclear War,* pp. 32, 34.

12. John Bennett, *Nuclear Weapons and the Conflict of Conscience,* p. 41.

13. Walzer, p. 279.

14. Walzer, p. 280.

15. Walzer, pp. 281, 282.

16. Zahn, pp. 7, 8.

17. Strobe, p. 3.
18. Major General Kermit Johnson, "The Just War, Nuclear Deterrence, Its Rationale and Weaknesses," Speech at a 1984 conference: Moral Issues and the US/Soviet Arms Race, held in Washington, DC.
19. Rasmussen, p. 20.
20. Yoder, p. 64.

Chapter 7: Nuclear Deterrence

1. Alan Geyer, The Idea of Disarmament!: Rethinking the Unthinkable, rev. ed., (Elgin, IL: Brethren Press, 1985), p. 28.
2. W. H. Kincade and J. D. Porro, Negotiating Security: An Arms Control Reader (Washington, DC, 1979) in The Challenge of Peace: God's Promise and Our Response: A Pastoral Letter on War and Peace, May 3, 1983, National Conference of Catholic Bishops.
3. Alan Geyer, Speech at Wesley Theological Seminary to an ethics class, Oct. 24, 1984.
4. The Challenge of Peace: God's Promise and Our Response, A Pastoral Letter on War and Peace, May 3, 1983, National Conference of Catholic Bishops, p. iv.
5. The Challenge of Peace, p. iv.
6. Geyer, The Idea of Disarmament!, chapter 1.
7. Geyer, The Idea of Disarmament!, p. 33.
8. Geyer, The Idea of Disarmament!, p. 60.
9. Geyer, The Idea of Disarmament!, p. 60.
10. The Challenge of Peace, p. 50.
11. The Independent Commission on Disarmament and Security Issues, Common Security (New York: Simon and Schuster, 1982), pp. 43–44.
12. Common Security, pp. 44, 45.
13. Ambassador James Wadsworth, The Saturday Review, July 28, 1962, quoted in The Idea of Disarmament!, p. 60.
14. Council for a Livable World, "Space Weaponry: Anti-ballistic Missile and Anti-satellite Weapons," September 1984 newsletter, p. 1.
15. The New York Times, Feb. 5, 1985.
16. Robert Bowman, Star Wars: Defense or Death Star? (Potomac, MD: Institute for Space and Security Studies, 1985).
17. Bowman, p. 92.
18. Geyer, The Idea of Disarmament!, p. 28.
19. Dale Aukerman, Darkening Valley: A Biblical Perspective on Nuclear War (New York: The Seabury Press, 1982), pp. 132, 133.
20. Robert Aldridge, The Counterforce Syndrome: A Guide to US Nuclear Weapons and Strategic Doctrine (DC: Institute for Policy Studies, 1978), p. 73.
21. Aldridge, p. 73.
22. Covenant for Peace, "Cruise Missiles: WIlliams International and Peace Conversion."
23. Common Security, p. 71.
24. Geyer, The Idea of Disarmament!, pp. 53, 192, 193.

Chapter 8: Alternatives to the Nuclear Arms Race

1. Eve Marriam, *The 1983 War Resisters League Calendar and Appointment Book,* Maris Cakers, editor (New York: War Resisters League, 1982).

2. The Program on Nonviolent Sanctions in the Center for International Affairs, Harvard University, 1737 Cambridge Street, Cambridge, MA 02138 (617) 495-5580.

3. Center for Conflict Resolution, George Mason University, 4400 University Drive, Fairfax, VA 22030 (703) 323-2038.

4. Interhelp, P.O. Box 331, Northhampton, MA 01061, (215) 586-6311.

5. "Berkeley Schools Teaching 'Nuclear Peace'" in *Los Angeles Times,* March 5, 1984, p. 3.

6. Bowman, chapter 6.

7. Bowman, p. 89.

8. *New Creation News,* Volume 4, Number 4, p. 5.

9. Association for Transarmament Studies, 33636 Lafayette Ave., Omaha, NE 68131 (402) 558-2085.

10. Gene Sharp, *Making the Abolition of War a Realistic Goal,* (New York: World Policy Institute, 1980), pp. 9, 10, 14.

11. "Civilian-Based Defense: A Short History" (n.d.), by Association for Transarmament Studies.

12. *New Creation News,* Vol. 4, No. 4, p. 6.

13. *New Creation News,* Vol. 4, No. 4, p. 7.

14. *New Creation News,* Vol. 5, No. 1, p. 2.

15. John Bennett, in *Christianity and Crisis,* Aug. 13, 1984, p. 301.

16. "Journey of Reconciliation to the USSR and Eastern Europe," *Michigan Christian Advocate,* Sept. 12, 1983, p. 8.

17. "International Peace" in *Windstar Newsletter/Products Catalog,* Fall/Winter, 1984, p. 1, 2.

18. Bowman, p. 79.

19. *Common Security,* p. 12.

20. *Common Security,* p. viii.

21. *Common Security,* p. 6, 8.

22. *Common Security,* pp. 8-10.

23. *Common Security,* pp. 139-141.

24. Sanford Gottlieb, *What About the Russians?* (Northfield, MA, Student/Teacher Organization to Prevent Nuclear War, 1982), p. 151.

25. Robert McCan, Wesley Theological Seminary Lecture, April 12, 1984.

Chapter 9: Plans for Action

1. Lawrence Romorini, "Peace Is Not a Season," in *United Methodist Reporter: Circuit Rider,* December 30, 1981.

2. "A Covenant with God" in "Peace Advocate Update," Winter, 1985.

3. "A Guide to Effective Letter Writing on Hunger Issues," Available from Bread for the World, 802 Rhode Island Ave., NE, Washington, DC 20018.

4. "Nuclear War Prevention Kit, 1982" Available from Center for

Defense Infomation, 122 Maryland Ave., NE, Washington, DC 20002.

5. "A Guide to Effective Letter Writing on Hunger Issues."

6. "Visiting with Your Member of Congress," Available from Bread for the World.

7. Carol Cory, "Peacemaking Tools for Our Congregation," Available from Discipleship Resources, P.O. Box 840, Nashville, TN 37202.

8. Joe Walker, excerpt from Sudbrook United Methodist Church *Newsletter,* September, 1983.

9. John Cogley, "A World Without War" in *The Moral Dilemma of Nuclear Weapons,* by Worldview (New York: Council on Religion and International Affairs), p. 29.

10. *The Challenge of Peace,* pp. 90, 91.

11. Jim Wallis, "The Work of Prayer," reprinted from *Sojourners,* March, 1979.

12. "Signs of Peace: Bonds of Peace," Available from Discipleship Resources.

Postscript

1. Aristotle, *Nichomachean Ethics.* Cambridge: Harvard University Press, 1945.

2. Bruce Birch and Larry Rasmussen, *The Predicament of the Prosperous.* (Philadelphia: The Westminster Press, 1978), p. 33.

3. Nicholas Wolterstorff, *Until Justice & Peace Embrace.* (Grand Rapids, MI: William B. Eerdmans Publishing Co., 1983), p. 161.

4. David Hollenbach, "A Prophetic Church and the Catholic Sacramental Imagination" in *The Faith That Does Justice,* ed. John C. Haughey, (New York: Paulist Press, 1977), pp. 258, 259.

5. Robert McCan, *World Economy and World Hunger: The Response of the Churches.* (Frederick, MD: University Publications of America, 1982), Chapter 1.

6. Stanley Hauerwas, *A Community of Character: Toward a Constructive Christian Social Ethic.* (Notre Dame: University of Notre Dame Press, 1981), pp. 73, 74.

7. Nicholas Wolterstorff, Chapter Six.

8. John Haughey, *The Faith That Does Justice,* p. 2.

9. Stanley Hauerwas, *The Peaceable Kingdom.* (Notre Dame: University of Notre Dame Press, 1983), p. 104.